Gentlemänly Repöse

Gentlemänly Repöse

CONFESSIONS OF A DEBAUCHED ROCK 'N' ROLLER

Michael Ruffino

CITADEL PRESS
Kensington Publishing Corp.
www.kensingtonbooks.com

CITADEL PRESS BOOKS are published by

Kensington Publishing Corp.
850 Third Avenue
New York, NY 10022

All Kensington titles, imprints, and distributed lines are available at special quantity discounts for bulk purchases for sales promotions, premiums, fund-raising, educational, or institutional use. Special book excerpts or customized printings can also be created to fit specific needs. For details, write or phone the office of the Kensington special sales manager: Kensington Publishing Corp., 850 Third Avenue, New York, NY 10022, attn: Special Sales Department; phone 1-800-221-2647.

First printing: November 2004

10 9 8 7 6 5 4 3 2 1

Printed in the United States of America

Library of Congress Control Number: 2004106175

ISBN 0-8065-2626-2

To my mother—for not reading this book.

And for The Cause.

I think a man ought to get drunk at least twice a year
just on principle, so he won't let himself get snotty about it.
—Raymond Chandler

I like to keep a bottle of stimulant handy in case I see a snake,
which I also keep handy.
—W. C. Fields

CONTENTS

ACKNOWLEDGMENTS

Without William Monahan this book would not have been possible. I also blame John Strasbaugh and Steve Hutton, but might not have, had it not been for the inordinate patience of Jeremie Ruby-Strauss.

INTRODUCTION

I attribute great piles of aphorisms more or less randomly to Dylan Thomas drunk at the White Horse, and this one recurs lately: Thomas, having another crack at the whiskey record, is dragged into a conversation with a student admirer who says he is writing a screenplay. Thomas says, "Good. Neither am I."

When I go around to the bars these days and it comes down to (God forbid) telling anyone what I'm Doing (as opposed to doing, which is drinking something), I sometimes refer to having been "working" a lot, or say that I'm popping in for one before I get back to the "grindstone." This is a mysterious thing to say because the sum of what I am known for locally prevents reference to "working" in any context but comic fantasy. So I protract: In place of the latest elaborate police abduction scenarios (however true), or telling people that I'm studying for the bar (this joke is especially lost on lawyers), or most likely saying very seriously, "*Nothing*," I have with increasing frequency just told the truth, which is that I am writing a book. And always, a little voice in my head says, "Good. Neither am I."

Inevitably, "What's it about?"

Well, I'm sure the theme of grandiose dispossession is obvious enough. But then it is the most prominent feature of the early-twenty-first-century vista (as well as the twentieth, nineteenth, and so on). Dispossession is right now enjoying quite a fully realized boom in fact; whole new markets are opening up all over—China, for example, and Saturday nights. Accordingly, there are few moments in this book free of someone being blackballed handily by the Fates, and I don't think I need to explain that this is not a contrivance. Basically everything is right out fucked most of the time. Should I stumble upon anything to the contrary, I will try to include it. So far however, the forecast is not looking up.

As for the "rock and roll" part, you will notice that the least-known band (exceptions noted) named in these pages is the . . . how shall we say . . . protagonist. I would love to assign a greater value to the band itself, maybe by exaggerating our record sales or by not leaving out all the supermodels and Caspian princesses we fucked. (Repeatedly. In castles.) I also considered changing the names entirely—not only to protect the guilty, but also to illustrate the point (maybe to myself) that it doesn't really matter. The same goes for the drinking and the drugging and whatever else. None of that matters—assuming there's a point. But there isn't, so it does.

While drugs and at least some rock and roll are herein pretty well covered, where sex is concerned, you will find this book lacking graphic examples. If you need bits about people urinating all over each other and shoving bananas into themselves, you know where to get it. This book will be no closer to *Tropic of Cancer* than the Tropic of Cancer is to New England. So if you must, insert at will a shot of the door of a luxury berth being kicked shut with light treachery and champagne; any knavery following will remain to be pondered, decorously.

Also there is no real dirt here to speak of, just filth.

I just went out for a look-see and a double bourbon. I thought I might come to some conclusion about this *Introduction*; that some giant *point* would come if I had a double bourbon. It didn't, so I had another. Then the bartender bought me one (as if I would be able to pay for the others), so I had that. Still nothing. Went and bought some gum. Came back and cracked a bottle of Calvados. Killed half of it, still nothing; opened the wine and now I am reminded of another Dylan Thomas story, which will be playing the part of the climax of the dramatic arc tonight: The intruder épée-ed through the drapes.

Dylan Thomas was hired, wisely and also unwisely, by the Guinness people to invent the end-all slogan; and to do so, if possible, overnight. He agreed, but would require several cases of Guinness and a private room at a nearby inn. For two days, anyone approaching (especially, one imagines, persons from the agency whose cowering steps he could surely identify through any door, in any state) heard the sound of exploding furniture, shattering glass, and unintelligible baboon-Welsh tirades. On the third day, the fire brigade kicked down the door. They found a *one Mr. D. Thomas* face down in an inch and a half of his deepest sauces, gesturing meekly towards the wall, where it was scrawled in lipstick, "Guinness Gets You Drunk."
Exactly.

Northampton, Massachusetts

Part I

Wunt Dunt Dunt[*]

*This is the title of a demo tape foisted on the Boston sub-urbs in the mid–late eighties by an inhumanly dedicated local death metal band called Toxic Narcotic. The tape contained four meticulously self-produced songs, one famously called "Silence = Death So Shut Up And Die." T.N. is as crucial to the annals of heavy metal as anybody.

Autumn Leaves

Fallen Angel

"It goes *danh danh danh dunh dut dut danh. Kill your mother or we will, Kill your mother or we will, Kill your mother or . . . me an' Ed will.* Then there's a fuken *sick* solo. It's called 'Kill Your Mother or We Will.' It's gonna be a fuken *hit*." The skinny Mexican kid went on about this new song he'd written. Paquito looked like a police sketch of young Mephistopheles. The baking tin of pig parts in front of him had been meticulously customized; he'd unstrung the muscle tissue and pinned each sinew down to make an intricate and morbid hammock, in which he placed the piglet's organs. He had also sliced off the snout and perched it atop two pencils. For the finale, he was now drawing the scalpel across the pig's neck, very much in spite of the mandate handed down earlier by the teacher.

As I watched the head pop off, I wondered about the people who chose to dissect the pig rather than the worm, and I further speculated that we would see Paquito foully puppet the severed head momentarily. The teacher was "conferencing" outside in the hall ("conferencing" meant smoking). So the piglet head lived again, and when all the girls were successfully climaxing with disgust, Paquito, satisfied, came back to his point.

3

"Me an' Ed got a band, but we need a bass player. That kid over there said you play." I looked over at my "agent," who was at the moment earning his twenty percent by making a gurgling sound and pushing a savaged piglet into Quiet Girl's face.

"Yeah. Not that well, though."

"He says you can play Rush."

Quiet Girl, now not so quiet, shot hysterically into the hall to find the teacher.

"Kind of."

"You shouldn't play that shit. It's gay and it sucks. You should join our band. We rule. We're called Fallen Angel. That's the *fuken* best name, so that's what we're called." He threw the goats, and then started planning shit at me, sounding utterly reasonable. He's got his cousin's friend at the radio station, we can play over at Ed's because his mother's never home, and among other things, he's concocted a fairly plausible caper intended to bring in a fuken sick set of Tamas. A terrible formaldehyde ache gripped my right eye.

The worm is thrashing furiously, mirroring my struggle to understand why I was required to dissect it. I mean, look—there is *nothing* in a worm.

"Do you know 'Autumn Leaves'?"

"What's that?"

"Never mind. We'll teach you it. We do it *sick*."

To this day, I don't know what "Autumn Leaves" is (the one Fallen Angel played anyway), and going over it with Paquito and Ed thirty times a week did not bring me any closer to recognizing it. Then again, "Autumn Leaves" was not the point, and luckily not all that requisite to joining Fallen Angel. What was requisite was perceived sickness on an instrument and the repudiation of all that was not metal. Ed, with a joint behind his ear, confirmed this in the hall after class. He added further that Fallen Angel was going to be the biggest metal band in the world ever. By Christmas. Well, obviously.

Metal Homes & Gardens

Ed lived four doors down on the right in an aqua ranch house. The grass was not in good shape. There was a tricycle jammed halfway up in the bush by the front steps. I am not positive Ed had parents. I went in there and Kiss was flashing in the dark room on an ancient television. Gene Simmons was pounding his fist on the hatchet bass and posing with the fake blood dripping off the cow-tongue. Irrelevantly, it sounded like shit. Ed, who was the hairiest person I had ever seen and who had been crafted by endless meatball sandwiches, was down with Kiss. He was just toeing the Fallen Angel party line when he turned Gene Simmons off as Paquito walked in. Kiss was not heavy enough for Paquito's Fallen Angel. Vomiting fake blood was acceptable, but Kiss didn't sing about killing people or things, which is gay.

Ed had a half of a drum kit with eleventy daddy longlegs on it under the basement stairs—barely half a drum kit really, maybe take away half of that again. Whatever portion, it had to be under the stairs because it was there provided the most secure way of suspending the pot lid for use as a ride cymbal. That very first time we played, Paquito was singing into the Mr. Microphone (something bad had happened to the birthday Peavey) about dismembering the corpse of somebody-or-other's mother when the pot lid flew off and caught him on the forehead, opening a gushing head wound. It was observed by Ed that it was like Kiss, but less gay. And so Ed was punched by the hemorrhaging Paquito and practice was aborted due to the pressing need for stitches. Next practice someone opened up the basement door and chucked a broken appliance down the stairs, knocking out one of Ed's teeth, so we moved things over to Paquito's.

There is little I would not do to have a copy of the flyer for Fallen Angel's debut gig. The Auguletto brothers invited us to play in their living room for their Super Bowl party. They were giants. Tony Auguletto claimed he used to beat the shit out of his father, who was the only person I have ever seen who was bigger than Tony—except for Tony's younger brother, who outhulked both of them. They had weights and muscle-developing machines in every room. I had been at their house twice before, and both times Tony Sr. pulled spot-checks to find out how much each of his fag sons was benching.

So sometime in mid-January, Paquito drew up this flyer for game day at the Augulettos' depicting absolutely incredible carnage. The body count he fit into eight-and-a-half by eleven inches was remarkable, with room left for about a hundred lightning bolts and directions to the house. There was a freshly chainsawed football guy in the lower corner whose expression captured a pain that could only be contemplated by Beelzebub himself. It was a great work. He hung it in the basement on the spare fridge so we could dig it while we worked on our chops.

Paquito's basement was more comfortable than Ed's spider farm: a linoleum palace with couches and bulk cases of root beer, where I was once again being spirited through "Autumn Leaves." Both guys insisted we were playing it right, but I'm pretty sure not. It sounded really bad, maybe even evil—perhaps there was a method there, perhaps not. Either way, it was going to get played for people, and they would love it. There wouldn't be a dry seat in the house. I cannot say I feel the need to enumerate the rest of the "set list" entirely. I'll leave that to the Internet fan sites. I will say that in addition to "Leaves," we were preparing renditions of "Fade to Black" and "Peace Sells . . . But Who's Buying" (commissioned by the Auguletto brothers). There was the new number penned by Ed called "Any Boo Will Doo." Another masterpiece. To "Kill Your Mother or We Will," my name had by now been added, as in *Kill your mother or me an' Ed an' Mikey will.*

Mexican Brothers of Metal and Their Mothers

Paquito's mother, his muse and sworn mortal foe, was a small Mexican woman in an apron holding a pan. She had no idea from English, and was metaphysically baffled by Heavy Metal, and therefore by her son. She might have been more frightened of everything if she understood a word of the murderous rants coming from the basement. The confusion had her basically at capacity. When it got to a certain point, she stood at the top of the basement stairs and banged her pan on the railing and screamed, "Paquito! Paquito! *No me gusta! No me gusta!*" This happened often, so we had to schedule band practices during one of the six periods of the day when she was at church. Even so, she was always already home and happening with the pan, with the Host still on her tongue. "*No me gusta! Basta! Basta!*" This would not stand with the gig crunch on. "Ma! We can't stop! *Tenemos un gig! Bitch.*" So we moved things farther away from the kitchen (from which the Señora emerged only to sleep in her immaculate shrine of a bedroom), into Paquito's bedroom. He put a dozen little eyehook locks on the door to create a temporary stronghold, and then during the next practice added a fuken sick deadbolt to keep her out. After he turned the last screw, he stood back and threw the goats at it.

Where the new room was concerned, security was foremost, though it bore us luxuries: wall-to-wall carpeting, for example, so that Ed's bass drum (he had gotten a cheap drum set for Christmas) wasn't lolling around like it did on the linoleum downstairs. The kit was in fact so solid that Ed was moved to add a drum solo to the middle of "Kill Your Mother" (Paquito had him cut it down to about eight minutes). There was a good deal of the usual ghoulish metal shit on the walls, with a Van Halen poster mixed in for measure. Even though Van Halen was to date short on songs about killing mothers, Paquito had drawn a little picture underneath the poster of Eddie Van Halen triumphantly ramming his guitar fatally through Yngwie Malmsteen's chest. Also, the room was warmer than the basement, and had a window.

C.C. Edster Goes and Does It

Ed one day soon produced a most unusual document. It was an official notice certifying his name change to "C.C. Edster." He had evidently *not* been kidding. Ed had a stew of invented names in his head, and he would stick a fork in there every few days and pull out the next thing you were supposed to call him. The gristle that stuck was this "C.C. Edster," so he finally took off his meatbib, threw his napkin to the seat and marched down to Town Hall with a ten-spot from his grandmother and a sack of semirare coins, in the great pursuit to be just a little more like the guitar player from Poison, who was the only one in that band who was maybe not *that* gay. Paquito, not sure about Poison, examined the paper.

"What's the C.C. stand for?"

Ed improvised some explanation that did not have anything to do with the letter C. He was apparently no better prepared to justify his name change to his mother when he got home, and was grounded for some time. Ed was your man, for better, for worse, but definitely for certain.

The Game

A week later, C.C. Edster escaped his house with a five-foot deadfall into a menacing frost and we picked him up around back to go to the gig at the goombah football party. Paquito was driving, having gotten his permit and the spare keys three seconds before Ed humped his twisted ankle and his only pair of drumsticks into the backseat. We all planned out which unspeakably unattainable hot chicks in tight sweaters would be pulling angoras over their heads as soon as we were halfway through the ballad while Paquito negotiated the one-way wind into the Lower Falls area, very illegally. I was picturing this blonde from homeroom with her top off, her hair all crackling and static-y, watching me drink Jack Daniels out of a shoe. Ed, pardon me—C.C.— was talking about a cheerleader we knew to be, quite beside the point, borderline retarded. We were almost killed four times in four ways before we pulled into the Augulettos' cah poaht.

The only female at the house, and who would be at the house, was Mrs. Auguletto, in a fucked reindeer sweater. She was in the kitchen stirring minestrone for twenty; she paid little attention to the fuken best metal band in the world dragging their Peaveys into the teevee room.

The pre-game show was on the Magnavox projection set and we were directed with primitive indifference by Tony Jr. to arrange our "Metal World or whatevah," over by the credenza and shut the fuck up. As we poked in the cables, the backs of the identical haircuts of the male Augulettos gave no shit. All three were on the couch. Tony Sr. turns around slowly and looks at us, then back at Tony Jr.

"Who's this guys?"

"That's the band."

"The fahkin . . . what?"

"The band. I told you."

"You told me what. What fahkin band. I'm watching the fahkin game. What ah yoo? Fahkin stupid? Yar a fahkin idi-it. What."

"What. No. They'll play during the commercials."

Paquito was unwinding an instrument cable when that declaration put him into mortal shock.

"Yahr a fahkin idi-it."

"What."

"What?" He gave a smack to the back of his son's head. "That's fahkin what. A fahkin band?" Then to Little Tony Jr. "You know about this?"

"What. No. What."

He knew. He had said about the Megadeth.

Tony Jr. will deal with his brother's betrayal later. Right now he's getting it from Pop.

"How did you get to be such a fahkin stupit shit? Huh? Not by me. It's your mahtha that's how."

Fallen Angel is hunting for outlets.

"Don't think I can't heah you in theah, Tony."

"Hey! Hey! Did the soup grow a mouth? Huh? Mind'ja bizniss."

Mrs. Auguletto murmured something threatening.

"Is that stirring I heah?"

Silence and the sound of a spoon going around slowly in a pot: tomatoes, destiny.

"I thought so."

Cymbal goes over.

Tony Sr. looks at C.C. Edster with the filthy denim, and then looks at his son.

"You fahkin disgust me. Whad'joo bench tahday?"

"Three-ten."

"Bullshit three-ten. Three-ten. Fahk yoo. Get ovah ta tha bench, ya fag."

I go out the door into the cah poaht for a smoke with our man C.C. Neither of us knows how to smoke, but we have cigarettes and the notion that this is what you do. The Edster is bursting with ideas.

"Dude. When I'm comin' out of my solo . . ."

"Uh-huh. Yeah. I don't think there's gonna be a drum solo tonight, Ed."

"C.C. Why not?"

He's air-drumming. He's already lost in the beat.

"I just don't . . . think so."

"I got this whole fuken sick. . . ."

Paquito comes out eating a Dorito and wiping orange flavor powder on his Dio baseball shirt, and he says very professionally, "No drum solo."

But you can't keep a good man down, and C.C. Edster is three good men, so now with the artistic differences in the cah poaht.

I go back into the *venue* to tune up my bass and Mr. Auguletto offers me a Coors Light, which I grab.

"So whadda you guys play in yoah little. . . .?" He makes a circular hand gesture.

"Um. Well. It's mostly like ah . . ."

Kick off. Fahget it. The Augulettos are transported. They are not coming back.

Meanwhile, in the Metal World next to the credenza, to which Paquito and Ed have contentedly returned, metal begins. Fallen Angel has been transported also, but to somewhere very different with no footballs and plenty of bloody chainsaws. Paquito gets it going. *Wunt Dunt Dunt, wunt dunt dunt* . . . and a Coors can pegs him in the shoulder.

"Shut the fahk up!"

"Fahkin commercials! Play during the fahkin commercials! We're tryin to watch the fahkin. . . . Geezus! Awright?"

Mr. Auguletto *cannoht fahkin believe this.*

Ed: "Okay. So . . . when. . . ."

"Hey! Shut. . . . Fahhkk."

The room gets quiet. No one's talking. Fallen Angel is having some chips and shutting the fuck up.

Little tiny feedback. Mr. Auguletto *whips* his head around with a look.

Fifteen metal-less minutes later a Dodge commercial comes on. Flick! Eeeeett! *Wunt Dunt Dunt Wunt Dunt Dunt* . . . "*Kill your mutha* . . ."

No Augulettos stop us, but Tony Sr. cranks the TV volume as loud as it goes, which is just a hair louder than Fallen Angel's not so fuken sick Peaveys. *Dodge trucks are Ram Tough. Ram tough* . . . *Wunt dunt dunt, wunt dunt dunt* . . . *factory-to-dealer incentives* . . . *wunt dunt dunt* . . .

Mid-solo, the game's back and a spoon with sauce on it hits me on the hand.

"Jesus! Shut the fahk up! You fahkin . . ." said Tony Jr. throwing a chunk of baccala at the best fuken metal band in the world, ever. It was made clear during the course of the surprisingly thorough bruising of Paquito that followed that we are supposed to play only during *certain* commercials. "Like ladies' commercials an' shit," of which there are none during the Super Bowl. We should be a little more towards shutting the fuck up, taking a lesson from Mrs. Auguletto.*

*This is *not* the most ridiculous gig I ever played.

Middle Tony wanted his Megadeth song, which he got a half-decent two thirds of during an M&M commercial. Then, during a Gillette ad, shit went really sour.

"Autumn Leaves" was totally impenetrable musically, which I suppose figures into the blind *rage* fueling the eldest Auguletto as he came over the couch in slow motion like . . . well, like a giant who is going to murder the fuck out of everybody, beginning with the wonky metal band in his living room. Fallen Angel is going down hard in a cloud of flying salt cod. Dip slaps up onto the ceiling, a cymbal takes a nice hunk out of the credenza, and the debut gig is very fucking over. Thank you! Good night!

If You Kill Your Mother, Who Will Drive You to Metal Band Practice?

Paquito was a Brother of Metal with a clear and universally unsettling look—like a guy who'd be comfortable holding a half-eaten baby. Even when somebody popped him into a Christmas sweater and he sat there and had some chicken like a person, it was still the other thing with the baby. He always had a thin little smile which crept onto his face as he tucked his chin to his chest and glared from under his brow. It was more than any devout Catholic immigrant could possibly take. And so it was unknown to the best fuken metal band in the world ever as they were resplendently wunting and dunting in teenage bliss, that on the other side of the door, the palace gate with the fuken sick deadbolt, something was coming. And the deadbolt was, for sure, sick—just not fuken sick *enough*.

We had been going over the same riff for half an hour. Paquito had taken to hanging a blanket over the window to block out the gay sun of the Overworld. C.C. Edster was back to using a pretty dumpy drum setup with a pot on a broomstick, since his kit got whacked by Mr. Auguletto.

Paquito was going on in the usual way about which parts of the song needed to be further sickened.

"First part's sick. Second part, not that sick. C.C., you gotta listen to the fill he does one more time. Rewind to where . . ."

Ccrrrrraaaaaaacckkkk!!!!

The door flies off the hinges and into the room, collapsing Paquito's CD rack, throwing plastic and apocalyptic cover art everywhere. Paquito's mother was there, screaming in the doorway with the pan, but there was someone, *something* else in the room, moving fast. Way too fast. Metallica posters are flying off the walls . . . Something floats onto my face . . . I can't see . . . *Somewhere in Time* . . . Eddie the monster is torn in half . . . the window was uncovered and outside was getting in . . . Through the chaos I saw Ed trying to protect what's left of his drums from . . . that dervish there . . . I see now . . . *No way* . . . It's a fucking *priest*. He's in the full shit with the robes flowing and he's swinging a six-foot crucifix . . . decimating a shelf of *Hit Paraders* and ticket stubs (you couldn't swing a six-foot crucifix in Paquito's room without decimating a shelf of *Hit Paraders* and ticket stubs). He's shouting and sprinkling holy water everywhere . . . *It burns! It buuuurrrnnns!*

C.C. Edster and I are in the hallway under verbal attack from the Señora.

The crazed priest in the other room tore Paquito's thin brown hand—which had just moments earlier been *shredding* with majesty—from the doorjamb the long second before the priest began the incantations.

Barbeque Gods
Fallen Angel
Rock Music 101 10:00 A.M. 2:00 P.M. Classes
South High School Courtyard Concert

By Johnny Turner

I wood'na even been theah but I had fahkin detention any-ways so I sawr it out tha window. So. Heah ya go.

First up was the kids from tha music room. One of 'em was Chinese ah sumpthin. Drumma sucked. I was a fan ah theah earliah material really like ah "Runnin' with the Devil" an "Smoke on the Wahta" and "Ayahn Man" an shit. I mean why mess with pahfeckshun? But anyways Will's a fahkin wiiiked pissa gitahrist. He fahkin did that fahkin Beethoven song he's been practicing fah fahkin eva. I shit you not by himself. Fahkin sick. Unfoahtunately the pahticipation of tha band was not so welcome afta. Theah vehrsion of "Rawk an Roll" had an Ackilly's heel if theah evah was one in the uninspyahd drummin of the kid with the pawkit pratecta. I mean you gahtta have a fahkin monstah drumma fah that shit not a milk-drinkin nerd fahkin lookin at a fahkin music stand which is fahkin 'zackly what they had. Moah like "Don't Rawk an Roll." I'm gahnna fahkin give that kid a fahkin cherry picka he'll neva fahget next time I see him. But theah was a ray of hope yet as tha too pee em class took ovah. Then we were treated to rite away a betta version of "Rawk an Roll." Gism-head's drummin is way betta than the athah kid which is not sayin much but tha intaplay between Will's gitah werk and tha rhthm section drove this band to nevah befoah seen hites on "Kashmeah" and "Freebird." I'm not gahnna put mags on it but this band is awright fahr getting ya theah.

Next up was fahkin metal gods Fallen Angel. Today 'Quito was on fiyah. The opening numbah as usual was "Kill Ya Matha." Oh how I nevah tie-ah of that song. I have the demo version in my cah. It suffahs from poah prahducshun quality tho. Why bands refuse to progress up from the Realistic tape recoahdas to the Yoahx is beyond me but who am I. Just a humble reviewah. With the addition of the base tha sound was filled out way betta. Pahtly I think plus it sounds betta 'caus Edstah's drummin is getting way moah betta than befoah. I think the addishun of a real cymbal also adds to the prafeshunalism of this band. So it was with a renewed enahgee that the Angel slayhd us with the lawng-awaited new numba called "Any Boo Will Do" which is about booze which is fahkin awesome. Fahkin booze rules and don't these guys know it. They luve ta get fahkin shattahed and so don't I. To date I had only heard the song sung solo by 'Quito durrin a smoke-break frahm Language. Like he had to tell me that Ed wrote that. It's vintage Edstah un-fahkin-mistakeably C.C. But 'Quito's gracious like that. Credit weh credit is doo. It's hahd ta heah the werds right now cuz theahs so much fucken echo in the fahkin prizzin yahd out theah but you can heah a bit of Poison creepin' into the sound heah which is a nice balance with the dahkah ovahtones of "Kill 'Em All"-era Metallica. The real saprize of tha set came kertasee of an Anthrax cahvah which was not a saprize afta all on account they fahked it up roy-ally. Plus I gotta say they really fahkin kill the momentum with that atha fahkin song, whatevah it is. In concloosion irregahd-less of certain shoahtcummings, in my opinion we have in Fallen Angel the makins of a phenomenon not seen since Megadeth oah Helix oah T.N.*

*Toxic Narcotic

This paticulah reviewah was the beneficient of several hits off a Pinna Pete special passed through tha window and not a moment too soon as the next band was a fahkin trip if I evah seen one. The gitah playa has no chops whatsoevah. Fahkin zip. Sounds like a cat in a blenda. Worse than fahkin Jimmy Page Outride-ah. Not to mention two of the kids ah frum Noath. Not noamally sumpthin to put this reviewah in one's coanah. One kid's heyah is stickin way the fahk up. Theah like punks ah sum shit. What the Bahbakew Gods lack in technical expateeze and total sickness they make up foah in exooberance—and food. They brought a fahkin Coleman stove and theah takin oadahs between theah songhs. Well they certainly have chahmed 'em out theah an Pete's bringin me a hoaht dahg and a fahken patty. The fahkin gawth chick just attacked the base playah an she's slappin him—wicked hahd. She's a fahkin weeado. Now she's fahkin getting into it with the fahkin ah whatsername the hippie. It's times like this I thank my lucky stahs to have the job I doo. Well finally heahs tha bahbakew. Well I don't know about Bahbakew Gods but certainly a respectable treatment of meats heah. Tastes a little bit like gas, but what doesn't. And whatevah theah playin out theah it's pretty fast. So that's not too bad afta all is said and dun.

Ahright I got two minutes left heah then I'm headin' down to Chisolm's Pond cuz Dean White's havin a little pahty and in the opinion of this reviewah SoCo Mahbees and Mydee Heidi in my Titey Witeies ahr a fahkin pissa combo. Oh and know what else is pissa? Me hammahd in half a fahkin owah. Wanna know what else is pissa? My new schedule. Check it out: Homeroom, free, free, Math whatevah, free, Shop, free, free. Read it an weep.

2

Rock More

Mink

I turned my head slowly to the left and I could see a bad-
minton game through an empty Gallo wine jug lying in the
grass. The smell of barbeque. Sleep paralysis. Finally sitting
up, eyes adjusting. I'm destroyed. Where the fuck am I? A
solar eclipse above me—I looked directly at it. Goood
morning! Extreme retinal damage. Hungry? Yes, actually.
Also blind. I had awakened in the midst of a family barbeque at Mink's at one in the afternoon.

"Hi. Sorry."

Mrs. Rockmore was stirring some iced tea. "Not at all.
You looked like you needed the sleep."

"Yes, I did. Thank you."

Mrs. Rockmore was perfectly unfazed. As far as family
events go, one could not do better than the Rockmores.
They just understood. "Would you mind if I used the bathroom?"

"Help yourself. You know where the towels are, right?"

No. "Yes, thank you."

Nephews and nieces in water wings were running around
the concrete pool edge, shrieking. Even their small patter-
ing and splashing sounded like a kamikaze attack in a
metal shed. Mink was in the kitchen in the kind of floral
shirt that something might pounce out of.

"What . . . happen?"

"Weellll, we had a liiitttlle bit to drink."

"I just feel kinda bad about the lawn business."

"Oh, no no no! It's fine! Really! You know about the wrong house story, right?"

"What?"

"Ooooh. This is good. One night me and the hardest partying female on the planet decided to have a little something to *drink*. I'm not too sure, but I think we had . . . several? Almost sure actually. At one point it was time for Minky to toddle on home, *NOT THAT I WAS DRUNK*! Well—a little tipsy maybe. So I get to the porch just fine, some trouble with the key but it's okay because the door's open. So I go in, and . . . lo and behold . . . I couldn't make it upstairs to my *bed*.

"So I slept in the foyer. And I felt bad about that, because you shouldn't really sleep in foyers. So then, at some later time, I was made awake by a *policeman*. Why? Not my house. Not my house *at all*.*

"Point is, lawns are pretty fair game. Though, you might want to caaalll about that little situation when you get a chaaance."

"What situation?"

"You're kidding. You really don't remember?"

"Remember *what*?"

"No. You remember."

"*What*?"

"No *way*! You remember."

"WHAT? What did I do? What happened?"

"No?"

"*NO*."

"Wow!"

*Robert Downey, Jr., has also excelled in this field, by bringing to the table international celebrity, and making it to a bed.

"Oh, shit. What."

"You remember the gig, though, right?"

"Gig?"

The Rathskellar

Boston, Mass.

The Rat has a special beer called "Ratbrew." The Rat has no brewing equipment per se, but the Rat knows that secret ingredients abound in rock-and-roll bars that could make something a "brew." Invisible seasonings can be harvested from every surface and, combined with the contents of the spillage trough, some arm hair, and the dregs of a skunked keg of Busch, they can be served to starving musicians in lieu of their pay. Bands are offered thirteen pints of "Ratbrew" per member just for showing up. The alternative was to pay full price for real drinks, or you could choose to have nothing, for a nominal charge. Much Ratbrew was slopped across the bar.

Boston, prior to the present time (that is, way back when), was going as well as could be expected. Aerosmith had left a parting gift of a million or so grams of the cocaine they were no longer buying to be doled out to needy artists and politicians, and though it proved to last not nearly as long as was hoped, solidarity was not lost among the local addicts. Boston College was slated to lose its football team, which would free the streets, and there was still false hope in Chinatown. Gang Green, having won some sort of "Battle of the Bands" sanctioned by adults (meanwhile, elsewhere, GG Allin had been honored by the League of Women Voters), was succumbing to what would become known as a true Curse, but Boston still had the counterwizardry of Anal Cunt. There were still rock bands—you could see The Pajama Slave Dancers, for example. Other than that, The Unband was the only thing going, and we were a state secret.

We had played the Rat before, guaranteeing we would not again—that was the way it went in those days. We already knew that it was better to negotiate through a fictional third party, and we decided on a good-humored manager from Texas. A few dozen calls from him, and we had a gig, with a modest guarantee even.

Green Day had enough corporate muscle behind it to save punk rock, and so the weakened Beantown underground empire had turned out from all corners to bum loose change off one another at the Rathskellar and see the band that once opened for them. The woman at Shady Liquor Miracle who never asked age-related questions had been devastatingly absent earlier in the day, so I had no choice but to slum about the crowd with my empty flagon trying to trade Ratbrews for sips of real drinks and hits of pot. I was having spare success.

"What'd you say?"

"Beer. To trade."

"That's Ratbrew," the diminutive rock person said immediately. "Nice try." He knew something about Ratbrew because he was the singer in the J. Geils Band. Everyone else knew because of the odor of the stuff or the telltale warp of the cup. Finally, one deaf guy behind the P.A., who had lost his sense of smell, traded me a joint for the rest of my Ratbrew coupons. I slipped the moist cigarette into the vest pocket of my vomit-stained Brooks Brothers and went outside with a girl. She was wobbly and smeared with pink makeup and we smoked the joint, which was of course dripping with PCP. The girl and several of her personalities—all of whom also wore thrift shop furs in the summer—began talking about jumping over the railing and throwing themselves into traffic, which I did *not* want to see when I was high, so I went back inside, where a band was onstage doing the equivalent with its career.

In the dressing room, Mink was consuming the last of his Ratbrews, and the first of a slew of somebody else's. Mink, by dressing up as a great polar bear, made sure that this particular audience would remember us.

We played our set, and the reception here (as elsewhere) was not particularly warm, unless you counted the isolated showers of Ratbrew. Still, when the headlining band took over the stage, and we took over the dressing room, the majority of the Rat's unsponsored patronage shoehorned itself in with us, leaving the room half-empty.

It was a righteous boycott, though only in retrospect.

The Evening War On

The dressing room was an agglomeration of chainsmokers jammed close enough together to share vital organs if it came to that, and collectively had enough Marlboros to survive at least until morning. The club's management took steps to counter the desertion. It wasn't long before our door was shuddering.

"OPEN UP! WE KNOW YOU'RE SMOKING CRACK IN THERE!"

I think we'd know.

"UNLOCK THE FUCKING DOOR OR WE *WILL* CALL THE POLICE!"

Bouncers at places like the Rat never call cops. Or wait, am I thinking of the Harvard Club?

"WE DO NOT ALLOW THE USE OF ILLEGAL DRUGS IN THE CLUB! WE CAN SMELL IT! YOU ARE SMOKING CRACK! ATTENTION!"

I opened the door a sliver. The door burst open onto a

small girl who would later have a hit song based on an imaginary letter to her mother, and her drink was a total loss.

"WHERE'S THE FUCKING CRACK!?!"

Yes. That is the question.

Cigarette smoke whorled out into the room where the singer of the J. Geils Band was not drinking Ratbrew. An interrogation of dressing room people by the two bouncers and the stupidest bartender ever had gone too far. No one wanted to be there in particular, but damned if any of these crazed addicts were going to be kicked out of the *shit hole* for *not* smoking crack.

Chaos erupted, with fists. Satan, a dealer, was dealt a blow with a chair. The emergency exit sounded. Mink, between species, was exploded into a drum set, scattering up a bucket of fish-beer. Two vampire girls threw their playbills to the ground, and headed for Uno's.

A college radio personality was thrown across the bar, and took full advantage of being back there while the battle raged. He was kicked in the ribs while paused underneath an open tap, and began throwing up blood, distraction enough for me to slip out and get paid.

At the top of the stair stood the man in the red ascot, sixty-something, rancorous and handicapped like Ian Fleming might have it. The ascot covered a notorious radio-era laryngectomy. Midway through introducing myself on approach from the second landing, I was re-ambushed and pinned to the wall, where I withstood two quick shots to the stomach. The bouncers then hauled me up in front of ascot guy. He was a villainous archetype: Dr. No Fucking Way. I demanded to be paid. He reamed me out from his *depths* through the voicebox. I repeated: We *need to get paid*. He was threatening me, distorting. I demanded to be paid. I was on PCP, and loads of it.

I was then cartoonishly ejected onto the sidewalk. After

how long I don't know, but before I could get up off the ground, one of the bouncers kicked me one more time for good measure.

Exercise Your Demons

An hour later, a much worse situation had developed. The *equipment*, most of which was not lost to anyone but the band from which we'd borrowed it, crossed my mind as the Buick disengaged its muffler rollicking over the meridian. (I would not see my bass guitar for three years.) I abandoned the car at a Denny's off Storrow Drive to pound out the rest of the chase on foot. I had identified a certain dread, and therefore been freed of it. It's good to get out and exercise.

Gig

Hadley Pub
Hadley, Mass.

An archbishop in Cork, Ireland, gave me this etymology of the word "gig." In the past, traveling bands in Ireland used to depend on the kindness of priests—in the same way that our band depends on bitter porn addicts and half-queer middle-aged men—to provide halls to play. So when things were going well, like if you got some food, you would say that God Is Good. G.I.G. Then—it being rather tiresome to be always speaking in capitals with periods between them— you say "gig." Probably the archbishop had it right, he seemed like the type. Though in the heads of the minstrels, lying awake on pestilent haystacks with only their gruel and infections, "good" was likely switched out for "gone."

The rain was crashing up from the road, spraying the backseat, soaking the equipment, and causing me to worry a bit that I would lose my grip and have a leg chewed off by Route 9, whipping along like a bandsaw ten inches from my knee. The Volvo was like a glass-bottom-boat ride in a very bad dream. The remaining six inches of rusted chassis bent down, caught the road, and sparked off behind us.

Everything was soaked, but we were tuned and ready to go at the No Man's Land Pub, to whatever end. The bartender washed glasses, and a farmer was looking at the hockey game. I think he was an *anger* farmer. The first chord was met with a coaster to my head.

"AFTA THE FUCKIN *GAME!*" The bartender, who hadn't booked us, walked out, unable to care less. The Anger Farmer grumbled.

"Little pricks."

3

House of Bastards

*These physical facts can not be disputed and are
sufficient to convince any reasonable mind that
we have been in the "time of the end" since 1799.*

—Harp of God, p. 239

Millennial Dawn

Someone was rapping on the door, unforgivably *antemerid-
ian*. Only zealots "rap" on doors—everyone else knocks.

The zealot did not like what he saw. In the greater sense,
however, he knew he had come to the right place. The
Bastard-at-Arms let him in and continued what he was
doing.

"Um. What's that you're . . . taking?"

"What?"

"I asked, what it . . ."

"What? Hang on. I'm gonna turn that down."

"That's better, thank you. No, I just wondered what . . ."

"Oh, this? This's just my medication."

"Are you sick?"

"Sort of. It's for my . . . ennui."

"Excuse me?"

"Actually, I'm glad you're here, um . . ."

"My name's Ken. Wow. That's a lot of . . . medication."

"Yeah, well—it's a lotta ennui, Ken."

Ken was still doing okay at this point. Still, he should not have come alone.

Ken was staring at a glass of *blood* and *alcohol,* in which someone had extinguished a *cigarette.*

A rag was aloft.

"So, Ken. Could you do me an enormous favor? Life-saving, maybe."

"Sure."

"Jam this into my mouth if I start screaming, okay?"

White Crosses and Chore Wheels

Ken, holding the rag as if it were going to explode, stammered.

"It's nothing to worry about, Ken. Just your name came up on the chore wheel, since everyone's asleep." Ken did not know how his name could have got onto anything in this terrible place, and doubted there was a chore wheel. He knew chore wheels.

"And don't, you know, *touch* it too much. It's kind of— whoa. Careful. Got it?"

"Yes. But what."

Ken stiffened. A person was lying in front of the refrigerator. The person could not at the moment be qualified with certainty as alive. "Is he okay?"

"Is who okay?"

Ken pointed.

"Oh. Him. I'm not sure I know who that is."

Ken was stunned. "Don't you want to know?"

"No. Why? Do you need something from the fridge?"

"But . . . is he okay?" Ken looked faint.

"Ken? You okay, man? Let's go in here and sit down. Watch that rag, all right?"

The living room—a drinking, drugging, smashing, and ashtray-dumping room, like all the other rooms in the most fearsomely debauched house in the world (there was a bar in the attic straddling the rafters)—was charmed. A six-by-six bay window with beveled edges, permanently cloudy with binge-film, covered most of the front wall. Broken televisions and computer monitors were strewn underneath the sill, and a sledgehammer. There was no earthly explanation as to why the window hadn't had a floor tom or a film student through it almost immediately, and the boundaries of the cosmos were so stretched now that the house had been quaking with bacchanalia for six months, give or take.

Today, the room was getting good autumn sun, and so was being literally ripped apart with light. A great cloud of toxic dust was galvanized in the jumping streams, and in this was a wood-glued chair containing a Jehovah's Witness named Ken. Ken was not comfortable. The only thing he could think of was this rag. It was suspended from his own trembling fingers. It was to be used in the event of a seizure. It dripped. It was soaked with an unknown and volatile liquid.

The Air Gun Idea

"So, Ken. What was it you wanted to see us about? You're not selling something, are you? Because . . . well, money's a little *tight* . . ."

The rag handler stammered. *Usually* they traveled in pairs.

"Hey. Fuck-fuck. Wake up. There's a *salesman* here."

Ken, who did not consider himself a salesman, protested unsuccessfully. Something shuddered on the couch. It had not moved, breathed, or otherwise showed the faintest sign of life. Achieving such deeply successful inertia would begin with Xanax, and include a funnel. Funnels were in high demand around the House of Bastards, being a comparatively safer way to rapidly introduce intoxicants than the air gun, for example. The lesson there, and everywhere, is to think *through* the idea, *all* the way through. To point, anguished screams of persons attempting to achieve the next level with a toy musket full of diet pills had been audible *through* last night. Around the world, many inspired food and drug administration concepts end badly.

The dark figure was up now, as if it had been all along waiting for the other things in the room to get up. It curled its claw around the nearest glass—a New England Patriots collectable containing an abandoned brown liquid and a drowned cigarette.

"You're early." It was talking to the Witness. "I thought you weren't coming till two."

At two-fifteen, Ken, in a shirt and tie, fearer of God and everything else, was being mistaken for a drug dealer. He could not understand this, and therefore didn't.

The creature took a whiff of the glass, paused, smelled it again and fished the cigarette out. Ken watched this from quite somewhere else. He was in the weeds.

"I didn't know I was . . . um, scheduled," Ken said.

"Oh, you were."

Ken shifted in the chair.

"Watch that chair there, Ken, it's—Ken! Rag!"

The rag was shockingly close to brushing lightly against the table and . . . Ken didn't know what. He jerked it away and propped his arm on his knee.

"Whew. Very close. Thanks. You know, if your fingers start to sweat, you should probably switch hands." Ken, saucer-eyed, did this immediately.

The couch creature was counting out crumpled money. It lost count several times and then tossed the scraggly heap of bills onto the table in front of Ken.

"So just give me the same amount as last week, of the mescaline, I mean. Not the other thing. That was fucking *obscene,* by the way. Fucking cramps were incredible. And give me the rest in whatever else you got. Oh shit, actually do you have any more of that fucking ... what was that ... ahhh. Fuck. You know. That stuff."

Ken did *not* know what stuff. Furthermore he was wondering about the person in the kitchen.

The bastard-at-arms was gesturing in an attempt to convey to the creature that Ken was in fact there to save people, but not in the good way. But prior to such time as a waking drug-beast has supped, it is easier to stop the tides than to get its attention. So the Bastard-at-Arms just said, "Percocet."

The creature clapped in recognition. "Right." That was not what it had meant.

Ken stared at the surface of the coffee table. Liquids of varied viscosity, wet cigarette packages fused to the glass and candle wax to its cheap wood frame; beer bottles filled with cigarettes, ashtrays filled with bits of beer bottles. The "coffee" table, for all its implied ass o'clock snapping of the *Gazette* and bright silences and nibbling on things which aren't pills, is awash in excesses too complicated to understand—let alone clean. Ken's eyes are just portals now. His pores have turned against him, open and emitting a *mist.* Jesus has left the building.

Ken swooned and gurgled as the chair collapsed beneath him.

"Ken! Rag!" Ken held the rag aloft as he and his book went over into a pile of filth. Ken was on the floor looking at the drug rag as if it were an *asp.*

The creature unsteadily aided Ken to his feet.

"You okay?"

"I should go," Ken suggested.

"No!" The creature had apparently developed a taste for Ken's companionship.

Second Comings and Goings

"I should go." Ken was trying to pass off the rag.

It was a changed creature that sat down. "It's all this . . . shit we take. And the fucking *drinking*. I think I might be an alcoholic." It gestured around the room. "It fucks us up and we can't *think*. Am I the only one who's *thinking* this?"

The bastard-at-arms answered, "True. We are *fucked up*."

"It's getting to be too much. I don't even know . . . I just. You know? Ken?"

Ken sat on the edge of the armchair. The Time was at hand (actually it was the drug rag. Ken was discombobulating—medically). The creature and the bastard-at-arms, having been jolted into drug sadness, continued. Ken nodded along sympathetically and was about to share the bad news that the world had ended, when—

"What the fuck was that?"

The creature froze. "What. Cops?"

"No. I heard something."

"Cops are audible."

"I think he's up."

The creature looked at its watch, which was not there and never had been.

Ken heard the sound more clearly. It sounded to him like a strike bowled into glass bowling pins, and then he saw an approaching monster dragging its leg—or a huge tail. Some action he did not notice soaked his pant leg.

"Fuck! Sorry."

Ken rose. He could not tell if his leg was burning.

"No, no! Please. Let me clean that up."

"It's okay. I can do it. I'm fine. I should be going. Really."

"No. I insist. Here sit." The bastard-at-arms went out.

The creature was kicking glass under the couch, lighting a cigarette. Ken coughed a little. "I really should be . . ." The creature, cigarette dangling, shoved him back down in the armchair. "Stay. We *need* you."

Iron Maidens

> *So remember who you say you are,*
> *And keep your trousers clean . . .*

The staircase produced another form. Paused by the window on the landing, the silhouette was unmistakably that of a certain *Mr. Hyde*, with a drink.

> *You schmucks all work for me.*

The creature was trying to do what one does with bygones, giving the frightened Ken a little *pep* talk, which meant he took more white crosses and said something.

"I'm really sorry about all this. I know we seem a little . . . disgusting," it looked up hopefully, for a sign on the face of the unreasonably detained Ken.

"Look who's here."

The bastard-at-arms had returned with a cocktail and the accompaniment of a Minotaur named Yeats, who was drunk. "This is Ken, who I believe I mentioned."

"Pleasure to meet you, Ken."

Ken, in a diplomatic collapse, examined his watch as obviously as he could. The sight of "Mickey" on his wrist comforted Ken, unaware that his wrist now belonged to The Mouse.

"So, turns out it's nine stitches."

"Let's see."

Yeats rolled up his sleeve to reveal the gangrenous mess.

"You sew?"

"I think so." Whoever it was had operated without sufficient lighting. The creature had some interest in forensics. It also knew something about bottle wounds.

"So what happened with the bisexual lass?"

Ken's face was curling up, discovering muscles even it did not know it had.

"She turned out to be three of them." Yeats exhibited a renewed interest in the wound, which was doing something that should be looked at.

The Witness's stomach turned.

"Ken! Rag!"

Ken tended to his drug rag with a practiced sweep of his other hand.

"Fuck you, two out of three were fucking *hosebags*."

The creature, satisfied, agreed. "Yes. *Two*."

Yeats drained the half pint and tossed it against the sill. There it was sluiced into a harmless pile of dirty broken glass.

"Why the *fuck* would you want to have three women?"

"Why would you only want *one* dollar?"

"Let me tell you something—"

"Please do."

"There are two things no woman in the universe will do . . ."

"What?"

"There are *two* things a woman, *universally*, will *not* do."

The creature, drifting back, rolled his hand forward.

"Listen."

"Yeess?"

". . . and shut the fuck up. Am I right?"

This was, actually, sweepingly agreed upon—in present

company. Everyone was sipping things and making silent exceptions.

"Why would you want *more* bullshit? I mean, what—do you have to make *three* phone calls now?"

Dr. Jekyll appeared, guzzling a fresh beer and managing an egg. Yeats looked distressed. "That better not be the egg."

"Fuck you. I bought this egg."

"You most certainly did fucking not."

"Fuck you. It's my *solstice* egg, and you know it! You didn't see the note?"

Dr. Jekyll changed the subject, "Any of you guys belong to that dude in the kitchen?"

The creature spoke for everyone by saying exactly nothing and lighting a cigarette. Ken, instead of leaping up, switched the rag hopefully to his left hand.

"That guy. . . ." Jekyll drained the beer, crushed the can and tossed it. "He's dead."

Fear of Sundays

"You remember last week. I mean, shit. We came this close."

"Fucking Christ, how the hell could I forget? Pardon me, Ken—*Jesus* fucking Christ. That's not something you just forget. "

"All right. Look, what's done is done. We have to deal, and if we wait we have a serious fucking problem on our hands. I think we all know what's at stake here." The creature knew something about problems. "Last week was a mistake that will not be repeated *this* week."

Ken was contraponambulating in sycraspaphy, and so he said nothing. It was all he could do, as through the doorway to the kitchen he had just witnessed:

Yeats heaving a deli slicer and golf bag onto the kitchen

table, the creature and the Bastard-at-Arms dragging a stressed Hefty bag out the door, and a total stranger striding through the kitchen with a chainsaw.

Wreck We Am

The International House of Bastards was not ultimately all that international, but bastards it had in spades. A regular bastard could be upgraded to a super-bastard just by spending ten minutes on the couch. It was of late-period Victorian pedigree, grey, sagging, polluted to the foundation. At times—sunrise—it looked like a tired Hun. It was six feet from the state road that runs between Northampton and Amherst; there were no turns on the drive out from Boston. An immolated teddy bear was impaled on a road sign out front. The house was rarely canvassed. The exception to this was the Jehovah's Witnesses, who were a constant inconvenience.

The house was the opposite of a production line, in that nothing ever left it intact. But this is not to say that the house did not *produce*. True, of the house procedures, few did not involve smashing something, and exactly none involved not drinking. There was a system, however. For example, we had an excellent job share program: You get a lot of job turnover in a household full of mouthy drunks, so if someone got a toilet-licking job, it wouldn't be long before he was let go, leaving an opening for another bastard; sometimes it worked out as a straight swap. Naturally, it was best if at least one person was involved in the food service industry in some unsupervised way, and in the beginning, while portions of the rent were still going out and there was still a wispy academic element to the house, we were flush with varieties of caviar, eaten on Spam, or spooned out with a Mickey's Big Mouth pull tab.

When the rent policy change went into effect, *Exile on Main Street* was epoxied to the turntable and the house erupted into an eighteen-month-long eviction party. By then, the little touches were hard to come by. We also lost our dental benefits and corporate discount cards. We still had food stamps though, sometimes, and there was a brilliant increase in smashing.

Joe and I once found a shipment of discarded computer monitors on the loading dock behind a computer store. Why someone would throw out perfectly good computer monitors, still sealed in their boxes, was beyond either of us, but the American consumer is fickle. Technology becomes obsolete so fast these days, we thought, as we lashed the whole lot onto the mules. There were so many of them juicy screens to smash, we had to have a party. We just changed "Victrolas" to "Computer Monitors, Many Varieties," and sent out the old invites. I believe it was Monahan who, with two Nat Shermans in his mouth and a Wild Turkey Old Fashioned balanced on his head, leveled a Hickory 3-wood at the last Par 5 Trinitron, and bashed it out of the park.

In retrospect, yes, we could have sold the 3-wood from the Camelot tag sale and all those monitors, and *bought* the House of Bastards, but fuck that.

I was under heavy verbal fire from a woman with Down's syndrome wielding a Lady of Fatima night-light. She was administering blows like a windmill—and she was, historically anyway, the reasonable one. She was shouting again.

"I'm embarrassed to see you!"

A Marshall 4x12 was being waddled over to a truck by the very very old woman who owned the house and the daughter with the glass eye who would own it soon. They were stealing every piece of our musical equipment that remained in the house, for collateral. A mid-sixties Wurlitzer piano and a homemade theremin were jammed into a rusty horseless carriage. They were stealing our *rock*. Cables, microphones, the only tuner we would ever own. The negotiations had broken down.

I had not eaten in several days, which was not unusual—but the intense malnourishment was taking its toll on me, as it was on everyone. We were confused, disoriented, depressed. Eugene and Mink had attempted to kill a cow the other day on the way back from the welfare office, but were chased from the paddock by an angry bull. I had chased a bunny rabbit halfway to Amherst, and would have kept on, but I was out of BB's. The air was getting thin.

The rent had not been paid in some time, and we had expected something like this might happen, but not having cars, protecting our assets was the thirteenth labor of Hercules. We had to physically drag amps, speakers, stereos, books, drums, a contrabass—everything—down the highway, all the way into town, and then go door to door looking for piecemeal storage spots in housing situations only slightly less tenuous than ours. We had been at it for days now, but it was getting heavy. A sheriff was coming any minute, and so everyone with warrants—meaning everyone—had disappeared, for good. Except for me. I was deflecting the blows of the *thwarted* young lady.

Doing the best I could, but I was weak, and soon I was against the tree, badly. All the instruments were gone, and earlier, I had lost a lot of blood.

This morning had been our Waterloo.

It began with the guy who came to read the meter, at about ass-o'clock or so. Critically allergic to sour mix, I was paralyzed beneath my typing table again, swelling up and struggling to breathe. Last night I'd had twenty whiskey sours during an Irish lock-in before I realized that I was not wearing my medic-alert amulet, and so was not protected. As I rose to see who was gasping with horror in the kitchen, I became alarmed by the sight of a great deal of blood in my room, which was unusual for that time of year.

The basement stairs had undergone massive strain from the coke-barrow at the party last weekend and would not take any more than a featherweight; a situation dangerous enough without the basement floor being a sea of broken glass, which it was, due to an innocent birthday tradition. At the House of Bastards, the person whose march toward death was being celebrated was allowed to throw a number of bottles equivalent to his or her age down the basement stairs, so long as it was not toward the area where the band practiced. Word spread and soon we were hosting more than enough birthday parties. Only once did we run out of bottles—someone had invited a tenured phrenologist and his life-partner Methuselah, and there was an unprecedented run on the furniture. We hired ourselves to play our next few parties, to help pay for new furniture, but we were real assholes about paying.

The stair, the meter guy, and his sandwich hit the basement floor—loud. Perhaps he was as substantial as his footsteps suggested, and was eating a rack of triceratops. Spinning toward the door to find out, I found the source of all the blood on the way to the floor. There was a three-inch gash in my side. It looked curiously like a knife wound.

The police had finished up their report and called the Board of Health, who arrived in yellow toxic removal suits and walked around the house commenting in superlatives. They tried to force my door open, but it was blocked by my silently draining corpse, and they satisfied their morbid curiosity with some kind of Geiger counter rod.

NORTHAMPTON POLICE DEPARTMENT

Police Officer's Incident Report

Incident ID#: XXXX
Incident Desc.: Open and Gross Lewdness
Date & Time Occurred: 04-10-94 0030 hrs
Date & Time Reported: 04-10-94 0045 hrs
D & T This Report: 04-10-94 1747 hrs
Principal Party: Eugene Ferrari
Address: xxxxx
City & State: Northampton, Mass. 01060
Phone Number: xxxxx
Dom Abuse (Yes/No): NO
Off. Writing Report: Det. xxxxx

Report: On 04-10-94 at approximately 0030 Hrs.
Officer Iago and I were conducting a plain clothes
detail in the downtown area of Northampton. At this
time we were conducting a check of the Baystate
Hotel for alcohol and narcotic violations.

The Baystate Hotel bar had a large crowd and a
live band was performing in the back room. An initial check of the front room located a subject who
had several beers in a backpack. These beers were
emptied into glasses and then drank by persons at
the table. I notified the Owner of the bar Mr. Snodgrass. Mr. Snodgrass acted quickly in correcting the
problem.

Officer Iago then approached me and advised me
that the drummer of the band which was on stage
was not wearing any clothing. I then went to the

back of the room and observed the drummer to be seated and wearing NO clothing. While the drummer played he stood up several times and played the drums. The drummer's genitals were clearly visible both while seated and while standing. The crowd was very rowdy and were engaged in "slam dancing." The name of the band playing was found to be "Unbanned."

At this point I decided that the smartest thing to do about the drummer was nothing. Any police involvement would cause serious problems for the crowd and the Officers. While making observations of the crowd I observed Mr. Snodgrass to enter the back room. He viewed the band members. Mr Snodgrass also made no action in correcting the problem at this time.

Officer Iago and I then went outside to the parking lot. From this location you could easily see the naked drummer. The drummer could also be clearly seen along the sidewalk along Strong Ave. At about 0100 hrs the band stopped playing. The crowd began to exit the building. At one point one of the band members looked out the windows which were directly behind him. He then chose to drop his pants and expose his buttocks to everyone standing outside the bar. I acknowledged this act and the subject did it again.

At this point Officer Iago and I re-entered the bar and identified ourselves as Police Officers. I then obtained the names of the band members.

The drummer was putting on his clothes as we

entered the room. I asked for identification and was
advised that his license was in his pants which
were in Room 1 of the hotel. This subject was later
identified as EUGENE FERRARI (DOB 02-08-71).
Northampton address listed as xxxxx. Mr. Ferrari
explained that he was playing music while wearing
a scarf which was pinned onto him. The pin broke
and the scarf fell off. Mr. Ferrari stated that the
crowd reacted to his being nude so he played the
rest of the set while wearing nothing.

The next person I spoke to was Mr. MATTHEW
PIERCE (DOB 07-28-69). Mr Pierce lives at xxxxx in
Northampton. Mr. Pierce stated that he exposed himself to the crowd outside because he "got carried
away." Mr. Pierce said that he directed the exposure
to Officer Iago and I. He stated that he obviously did
not know that we were Police Officers.

The third member of the band was identified as
Mr. MICHAEL RUFFINO (DOB 10-23-71) of room #1 of
the Baystate Hotel of Northampton. Mr. Ruffino
stated that he did not expose himself to the crowd.
He then showed me that he was wearing black
leather pants. Mr. Ruffino then explained that he
almost could not get into the pants, let alone get out
of them.

Mr. Ferrari and Mr. Pierce were both advised that
they were going to be summoned to court for open
and gross lewdness. Both subjects made gestures
and drew attention to themselves while in clear
view of the public, including members of the audience and passers on the City street.

Mr. Snodgrass was advised that an Alcohol Beverage Commission Violation would be filed on Monday. Mr. Snodgrass explained that he had NO knowledge that the band was going to expose themselves and he assured that the band "Unbanned" will now be banned from the Baystate Hotel.
Mr. Snodgrass stated that when he found out that the band member was naked he felt that it would have caused more problems if he had tried to stop it. Mr. Snodgrass stated that once the band is on stage he has no control over the band or the crowd.

Paperwork will be submitted for violation and criminal charges.

— Northampton Police

4

New Yuck Shitty

G.I.G.

Coney Island High,
New York City, c.1997

"So you guys get two drink tickets."

"First of all, the bar is closed. Second of all, there are three of us, and third, we can't buy gas with drink tickets. We've tried."

This was the part of the night called "settlement," where you handed over whatever you had left. The booking agent was pretending not to have known us for as long as she had—since back in the Boston days.

"Well, I suppose I can give you the cash equivalent, then."

"And how much is that?"

"Six dollars."

"Six dollars? You do *realize* that we live in western Massachusetts, right? Remember?"

"Well, okay, I guess I can do seven."

We were temporarily forced to now live in Manhattan, surviving on our wits and the kindness of strangers, mostly the latter. Gas was achieved four months later, but by then it was too late. The car had long since vanished. We had been pulled in.

Still Life with a Wolf

Captain Nightshade was a hero to those tangled in the World Wide Web, which has nothing to do with computers. He was a revolutionary of some repute who favored the gifts of foul unpronounceable jungle roots over conventional drugs like DMT, STP, or GBH, though those would do in a pinch. If he couldn't provide you with one of those, he would apologize, and synthesize something better and more deadly out of a sock and some secret berries. He grew belladonna in a retired chimney, aged frog poison according to ancient cuneiform instructions, and had a vital relationship with a full-grown gray wolf. The wolf was named Merlin because he could tear your fucking face off. When we met him, the Captain was running a small 'zine out of the most defensible house on the Connecticut River.

One day, The Captain was hosting a Hampshire College world music band and twirling away on LSD in the living room. The band was unpopular even though they were called The White Shadow. We watched them through hangovers from the kitchen until the Captain returned with his box. Today was Wednesday, and that meant Captain's choice. He opened the box and held up a baggie containing—well, we would obviously be throwing up for some time before anything good happened.

The Captain had produced the Dung of Quetzalcoatl, which was used by jungle tribes who had no televisions. The Captain took off his three-thousand-dollar pilot's watch, then began performing a routine but dangerous surgery on reality itself. He scrubbed, and then proceeded with the ceremonial coffee filter and mashing spoon and, as usual, a liquid which required him to use gloves and be silent. He put the dung in the microwave to render out its mind-altering nectar. We killed some time on the porch, drinking absinthe. It was a bright afternoon.

Some time later, after consuming nearly a quart of the most vile liquid north of hell, and after I vomited a whole organ onto the beer ball under the porch, I sat in a deep peace watching the Panzers roll up over the hill, crashing through a forest of totem poles and down onto the beach-head. I needed fresh cane for my drink and so slid open the glass door, into a room of frozen people. No one twirled.

"Don't fucking move." The Captain sounded very serious.

The music had been switched off, and thank God because it had been the Grateful Dead. A bongo-playing dirt-wizard by the name of *James* was backing almost imperceptibly toward the door holding a grocery bag, later found to contain several kinds of fresh raw meat intended for the grill. Even I could easily catch the scent—as a matter of fact, I could see it—whereas the wolf, its hunched shoulder a yard off the ground, could not so far. "More *legato*, please," requested the Captain. The carnivorous hippie James took right away to the instruction. James was a "communications" major, but his host knew things the way Tarzan knew them. Captain Nightshade, major communicator, knew that it would be best if all non-exiting persons remained perfectly still as Merlin stalked the groceries. Merlin the wolf sniffed the petrified freak-in for a very, very long time. *No one* can domesticate a wolf—this is to be noted in stone. The next time we saw the Captain, he was living in darkest Brooklyn, no wolves.

We had been drinking at a dive called Max Fish. It was a Monday, which is Saturday for serious drinkers. My last two quarters were invested in a game of pinball. Plastic aliens were rapidly jiggling, because I had just fucked up their mother ship. Out of the corner of my eye, I saw the sage who could turn anything into drugs. He floated across Ludlow Street. Aborting an exciting but hopeless multi-ball, I leapt into the window box and started screaming. It was another bright afternoon.

Following a brief recap of his time in the Peace Corps, Captain Nightshade provided a laudable narcotic pill of his own creation. It kicked in almost immediately. Over jiggers of atropine, The Captain announced that he was in the course of some experiments having to do with DMT.

The Green Grid

Since long ago swearing off acid, mushrooms, and being in rooms with persons on either, I have had little contact with the psychedelic world beyond what I can muster staring too long at bathroom tiles. DMT, however, described once (by the Captain) as the "bull's eye of psychedelics," appealed to me. So it went that one day in New York, my pocket held a Ziploc containing a fuzzy thing, and consequently the—very odiferous—mysteries of life. I was given surprisingly concise instructions on how to manage one of the most powerful drugs available in the world: "Don't drive."

I was anxious to reconnect with a lost dimension, and so placed a call to the nearest friend with a roof over his head and asked if I could use his bathroom real quick, as I needed to "pester God." He said sure. His girlfriend was holding some sort of dressup event with cousins, but I had it on good information that the heavy part of the trip would be over inside of twenty minutes (I think someone said that it was sometimes referred to as "businessman's acid"—or something like that). I'd be out of there before anyone suspected anything other than that I was having a tremendous *movement*.

I passed the smoldering crack squat and entered the extravagant and gleaming high-rise full of swank condominiums, where I was let into an apartment by a web designer. There were candles lit on the stainless steel bookshelves, a silken rustling, a baker's dozen of star-crossed introductions as I passed eleven Audrey Hepburns, a record company president, and a jewel thief, and I went into the bathroom. Locked the door, prepared the pipe, turned off the light and smoked the hideous thing from my pocket. There was a knock, and I heard myself firmly say "no." Things would be getting underway.

Another knock. "No," I said from under a relative stranger's girlfriend's towel rack. Nothing happening yet, so I took another hit. Another knock. "No!" But this knock hadn't come from anywhere on the Lower East Side.

"Come in."

Sixteen minutes later, I came to in the tub with a fistful of shower curtain. I opened the door onto the dinner party. Finding myself more or less adjusted, I managed a fairly scrupulous farewell, and left the apartment a completely different person.

Bull's-eye.

It's *That* Easy!

I was sitting in The Captain's basement apartment, with Mistress Cute-as-a-Button, a dominatrix who was as cute as a button and also was the band's primary benefactor at the time. We were in an area called The Laboratory. The Captain had a substitute for oxygen—"Air's what the Man wants you to breathe," he said. He was inhaling liberally from a six-foot tank with a clown painted on it while he made some preparations.

The Captain's directions for the strange road ahead were

exacting, but unfortunately, I missed a good bit of what he was saying because I had been drinking at Max Fish again for two hundred hours straight. He patted a jar next to him, an antidote of some kind, and Mistress Cute-as-a-Button was incredibly practiced at whisking me out of sewers before the C.H.U.D.s got me, so I went ahead and took the turkey baster full of drugs.

Terrible taste, nothing happened. I shook my head and looked over at the Captain. He was standing there with the emergency jar in his hand. "Didn't expect that. You all right?" He was somewhat concerned—empirically, at least.

"Fine. What." I was covered from the chest down in vomit. This was easy to discover. *But* it had also been necessary to chase me through Prospect Park, where a madman—in my clothes—was frightening people with serenades on an unstrung guitar. I'd read about him in the *Illyria Times-Picayune*, which I had picked up from the fishwife every morning for the past eight hundred years, even after the price went up two shrew heads.

Really, several months had passed, during which I had fallen and been helped up many times, eaten very little, changed my pants twice, charmed many women, been thrown out of six bars, lunched upstate, killed a man just to watch him die, rowed a boat in Central Park, spectacularly disowned my shoes, and lo, we had a record deal.

I'd Like to Thank the Little People

The other day, I heard a story about a metal band. It's best that they remain nameless, though one can only hope that they would take pride in these events.

This particular band, not ever terribly popular, is now named only on metal nostalgia fan sites. Back then, like many of their contemporaries, they were granted by their label a cautious budget to make a video for an impossibly bloated concept album involving enshrouded mountains and swords and lightning. Of course in retrospect, the basic failure here is that not only was the quota for this sort of thing filled some years prior, and not only was this post-Nirvana, but there was no way to have attractive women in it in an attractive way. Animal skins, tiger makeup, proximity to ghouls and armored horses, clawing around by torchlight—if that's for you then you're not Everybody anymore, which is why you have to make your video with shit from Lechmere's department store, and why you only get to make *one*.

This here video called for a dwarf to steal treasure off a dragon. Or a mountain king thousand-year-old sorcerer chap. Or something. At any rate, a little person is hired (I am not sure what we're saying these days to correctly refer to our smaller friends, or, incidentally, to anyone else) to come in for a five-hour shoot, at some tourist cavern, because they can save a few bucks on the production costs by renting out a place that already has eerily illuminated stalactites and bats. They've got the dwarf in the makeup chair for some eternal length of time, attaching all manner of prosthetics to him. It's the usual B-grade ogre shit. Nonetheless the role is visually extreme, an odious Middle Earth nuclear winter wonderland type. So there he is in his giant bat ears and fangs and—notably—a monstrous rubber nose.

The dwarf is doing his job, shoving costume jewelry into a potato sack and hunching and snickering and wringing his hands together, but the shoot's running long. There's some problem with the dragon or the bass player's having a conniption about pimentos. Whatever it is, time's up and they have to re-open the place to the tourists and shoot the rest tomorrow. Problem is the dwarf's makeup isn't reusable. Aqua-Net and blow and dragon expenses have already compromised the budget, so once he pulls everything off and wipes himself down, that's it. No doing it again. There's only one choice and the production team tells the dwarf he can't go to sleep. He's gonna finally go fucking SAG for the overtime, so he's amenable. Then he starts drinking. A lot.

By all accounts, after a couple hours our man's completely in the bag. He's belligerent and crashing around talking shit in full costume, swinging a bottle of something dangerously close to the ground. He's seen here and there leaning on a stalagmite, pointing venomously at tourists from Wisconsin and asking them what, exactly, they are looking at. He starts getting pretty tired, and then he disappears. The addled British video director, who has been for how long dealing with the trappings of a "serious" metal band making a bloated concept video involving enshrouded mountains and swords and lightning instead of working on a feature starring *anybody*, walks into the bathroom next to the gift shop for a piss, where the singer of the band has the dwarf upside-down by the ankles so that a member of the entourage can dump spoonfuls of coke into the rubber nose in hopes that some amount of powder will make its way into the dwarf's real nose. The arrangement of the prosthetics and the mental state of the people involved in the project made it impossible to conceive of any other way to keep the dwarf awake. The director, it is told, fucking snaps. The dwarf bolts out the door as the singer tries to explain things against a tempest of profanity and flailing arms and punching and stall-door-kicking. Meanwhile, the dwarf is loose in the caves, with a half-unglued troll face and claws and plastic armor, ripped on a gallon of booze and a level tablespoon of caucus powder, screaming and careening across the cavern bridges, swinging a sword.

Tourists are scattering and snatching up five-year olds, foam demons are fainting, lighting rigs are going down and park rangers are pouring in with no idea.

Now that's a *video*. Ours? Well, we had a monkey.

Hail to the Chimp

Word of the monkey signing on to the project arrived via fax from his agent. There was a dot-matrix-quality print-out of our man sitting in a chair with that sort of smile they do where the lips flap up. He's looking off into the distance and I think wearing an ascot. Someone had scrawled, "Here's the chimp," and drawn an arrow. Yep. There he is.

I've heard a show business rule to the effect that you're not supposed to work with monkeys or kids. Maybe it's true if you're an actor or comic, but this does not hold true in the music business. (Our equivalent is, until you are fucking *huge*, don't go on after a Japanese band and don't compete with sporting events.) Van Halen had Waldo, Twisted Sister had the yelled-at kid, we will have Chippy.

The whole monkey business began innocently enough with this cocaine idea about a bikini contest promotion we were "brainstorming" (drinking heavily) the night we got signed. I'm not sure exactly in which bar we were, but it was somewhere on the Lower East Side. We were drinking vodka with cranberry, as I had for some time been championing the notion that cranberry juice in large quantity would purify the blood and clean the kidneys, and we could be evened out after twenty of them. There is some truth to this. But. Our A&R guy, Lenny, and his tremendous girlfriend, who also worked for the label, are talking loosely about how it's gonna go for the next few months—calling radio stations, little promotional appearances here and there, getting on some nice little shows, and having a record release party. The last is where we weighed in with a plan to have a special contest where incredibly hot literate women must come in bathing suits. They would be received of course by a composed and mindful crowd. The winner and the second- and third-place winners would have the unique opportunity to dine at Balthazar with us and an orangutan, who, it was secretly expected, would get assholed on Pernod and go completely fucking jungle on the place. He'd be throwing shrimp and ice and balls of his own shit, which would leave us largely out of any unnecessary conversation and/or blame, except on Page Six.

I was really pulling for the orangutan as opposed to a chimp, because they're a bit more *continental* I think. You walk in to Balthazar Saturday night, VIP, limo, bikini contest winners, you want to one-up the hipster band who brought the overworked bonobo, and the folk guy with his macaque. Plus François might show a little more hustle with the drinks if your particular primate's two suit sizes up on a Le Car and can punch a hole in concrete. It's stupid, but so is the whole fucking thing until you actually do it, and then everyone else wishes they were as stupid as you.

Inexplicably, the idea was met with genial resistance in the conference room at the label, and bellowing outrage in the war room. Undeterred, we said, yes, we'll do a regular non-monkey non-shitball sort of party at Life, but when it's time for the video or anything, *a fucking monkey comes.* I should mention that I am really not too sure that everyone else was as dead-set on this as I, but when the fax came through to the home office, *everyone* laughed and cheered for hours and we put it on the refrigerator and got drunk to it. Have monkey, will rock.

The shoot was at a studio a couple of floors above the label offices, up an elevator to a white place where Mr. Johnny Production was *at.* He had heard the radio interview the previous evening during which we announced an open call for *ladies.* Mr. Production, listening in his stately Bronx digs heard the call, and he had *ladies.* Well, a lady anyway.

"Hey, yeah okay. This is niiiice. Yeah, not too bad, not too bad. Let me tell yoo sum'n, yoos guys. Yoos guys is a hundred and ninety percent."

"What?"

"Okay, nice to meet choo um Johnny Production, of Johnny Production Productions, this is Dina . . ."

"Hi."

"Hello."

"Good morning, Dina."

"So I heard your show and here I am, Johnny Production at your service. You just tell what you want my girl to do and BANG!"

The room jumped.

"She does it. Yoos guys mind if I have a little coffee from dat machine?" On the way over to the percolator, he relieves the buffet of one of everything. He pours a cup of coffee. He looks at me steadily for a second, mashing his lips in thought.

"I got one word for you," says Johnny Production, about to change my life, professionally and otherwise.

"*Stetson.*"

The morning progressed, it turned out, much as Johnny Production would have it. Girls were photographed with a cigar-smoking chimpanzee in Armani, and there was much to spirit away from the catering table.

Afternoon, however, belonged to the exasperated chimp, who ceased *behaving* in the middle of a scene. According to the storyboard, he was instructing us (he was, storyboard or no) while we all sat on a couch. All of a sudden, he went blank, and lost interest. The trainer's diagnosis was immediate.

"Okay. Five minutes, everybody!"

Chippy waddled off after her towards the lounge. He waddled back, seconds later, lumped himself back onto the couch, and opened his beer.

Not a Band

By Sarah Fim

For the love of all that is holy, please, PLEASE do not be tempted to purchase The Unband's *Retarder*, because this reviewer would not be able to live knowing that someone out there experienced such *torture.*

I never knew that three minutes could seem like a lifetime, but it does in the hell that is bad rock music. While each and every track on *Retarder* deserves to be ripped apart, there are only so many sarcastic, scathing comments one writer can dream up, so instead I will give you some song titles that are quite amusing and worth a few laughs. I'm sure it takes a musical genius to dream up such titles as "Cocaine Whore," "Crack Soundtrack," and "$#@?!!." Are you seeing a pattern develop here? After listening to *Retarder*, I have absolutely no clue who would ever want to run out to their local record store and blow seventeen dollars on this waste of a CD.

I have heard some really horrible bands throughout my life such as Fountains of Wayne and Chainsaws and Children, but The Unband just completely surpasses these two in terms of bad songwriting, singing, and instrument playing. If The Unband never accomplishes anything else in their pathetic lives, at least they will be known as the worst band in the history of the United States. Congratulations, guys!

—*The Chicago Maroon*
FEBRUARY 11, 2000

Part II

Nu-World Order

Being There

Day 3
Chicago, Ill.
Dokken, Great White, The Unband

We had this kid in junior high school named Don
Dokken. He was five foot one, ninety-seven pounds,
and his birth certificate said something different.
One day he was screaming from inside a hurricane
of rat-tails in the locker room, "I'm Don Dokken!
I'm Don Dokken!" You'd think that would only
happen once. No.

I didn't spend so much time in the gymnasium
myself—I had business in the woods. But I did see
this occur many times, and the thing is this: Fuck.
Leave the kid alone. You have enough on your
plates, Mrrs. Fullback and Tightend—you're gay
homosexuals. So anyway, suddenly, I have this irra-
tional empathy for Don Dokken.

Chicago is famous for its empanadas, mostly because of the unique portions (none) and the prices they fetch at the airport. Here at the House of Blues, the empanadas are *flowing like wine*.

What. Did the fucking country turn upside down? Why are there three kinds of empanadas on my fucking . . . thing here? What are you trying to do, give me a fucking coronary? Three? Who's in charge? I need to see the Khan. What? Fine.

What's that light? What's wrong with it? Is someone coming? Someone bad? Why does it blink? Wait. Did I tune? Oh yes. Of course I did, weeks in advance. Who's the man, me? Yes.

The light stopped. Oh right.

Here we—shit! Plug in!

Damn. How many fucking people is that? One, two, three, four, five, six, seven, eight, nine . . . ah, fuck that.

Man, it is fucking *hot* up here. I should bring an egg next time. Who does that, cooks an egg? Is it Alice Cooper? What is this now?

Wait. Wait. Are they *boo-ing*? Or is that *whoop-ing*?

Nope. That's definitely boo-ing.

Well hello, ladies. I love you too. Lord, this would be the *worst* orgy. Where *am* I? Oh yeah.

Did someone just throw a *Bic* at me? What. A *waitress* hates us too?

Hey. *Hey!* Check it out. I have an idea. After this song, I'll get the pyro ready. When I hear you go, "WHO HERE

LIVES WITH THEIR MOTHERS? LET ME SEE YOUR
HANDS!" I'll set off everything at once. Good. No?

What's that? A friggin note? Who writes a note? Lemme
see that.

5

Out in the World with Motörhead

**MOTÖRHEAD, NASHVILLE PUSSY
& THE UNBAND
U.S. Tour
September–October 1999**

What We Talk About When We Talk About Rock

If this whole thing blows up on us tomorrow and we have to go civilian, at least we will have the knowledge that we've done it all our way, albeit the hard, stupid way. And that we have the rights to all our greatest disasters. Well, not *all* of the rights, technically. The Sovereign of the Universe has a couple points, as does the production team of Anheuser-Busch and Rabid Impulsiveness, and a few more are held by a Puerto Rican gentleman on the West Side. And then—right—there's General Liquor and Headache Tablets, LLC, who have a good chunk of the publishing (we wanted to fight for a reversion clause, but a squirrel told us not to bother). There's an Exclusive and Permanent Licensing Agreement with a European pharmaceutical company which compels us to name-check Paxil at least six times on our next disc, and we gave up a couple points to Management—which we are told is in the hands of a giant invisible rabbit who runs our day-to-day from a mystical lair (oh, and one of the rabbit's alcoholic friends got the merchandising rights—whatever *those* are). Then the hopelessly enigmatic *mechanicals* are collected by the Society For The Protection of Neither Fish Nor Fowl, and naturally the Mob gets a sizeable tribute. (Or is it the Tongs?) We signed off on the Smithsonian thing with the future in mind, so the museum gets our livers when we turn thirty, and in the end, the whole bag may or may not be handed over to a girl in Duluth who owns us, in perpetuity, throughout the Universe. Yes, damn straight, we are the Captains of our three-chord legacy. So we have that—that and half a case of warm Bud.

San Antonio, Texas
9/30/99

Every time I come here, I just think of the first time, with the lone girl watching us improvise in front of the tinsel curtain for two hours. So we've already played our best show here. And even playing with one of the greatest bands on the planet in front of a packed house pales in comparison. I'm glad when things work that way. Like winter light hitting the rusted arch of a railroad trestle, or like when you have twenty dollars. What I mean is, when impossible beauty wins, it's nice.

Austin, Texas
10/01/99

The place is out by the mall. We hung around the load-in dock with Nashville Pussies for a while. They seem all right.

I think one or two of their touring party is on drugs. Unless I'm not supposed to say that, in which case everybody's fine and having a mocktail. Bass amp is fucking off again. I went to one of the stage guys at the club (for the three-thousandth time in my life) saying I don't have a bass amp. He was shockingly pleasant and right away fetched a Motörhead roadie, and together they attempted to fix it, with me looking on and drinking a free beer (the first of an announced "unlimited" supply). The quick repair job seemed precarious in the end, so the Nashville guitar tech chap comes in and loans me their amp with a smile, and says he can have my amp up and going tomorrow, no problem.

Jesus. That was really some fucked-up shit.

At the Bawdy-House

Dallas, Texas
10/02/99

Dallas, "Big D" (as opposed to Denver: "Little D") is home to Puss' uncle Rick, a born-again Texan who is putting us up for the night and letting us hang around the house while he's at work tomorrow. We parked the van, dumped our bags, downed a Silver Bullet each and were whisked to the strip club at eighty miles an hour in a red Sebring convertible. There was a pair of Chinese lions at the entrance of the club, one partially obscured by an easel announcing the arrival of a Woman of the Profession with endowments to awe God.

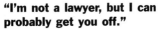

"I'm not a lawyer, but I can probably get you off."

We got seated in a semiprivate area near the stage and were brought rounds of drinks very efficiently because Rick was known in the place, and because his guests were limo-worn "rock stars" presumed to have cash and cache. Extra attentions were paid to us in the standard manner. At the next table, an attractive Asian woman in a thong was bent over at a mathematically pure ninety-degree angle, hypnotizing a slack-jawed captain of real estate with her ass, while she was otherwise engrossed in mechanically counting hundred dollar bills near the floor.

After that, we spent the remainder of the night on the back patio with a case of Coors Light firing a .357 into the woods, retiring to the wraparound couch only when we were out of bullets—both kinds. We didn't ask, but we were comfortable that Uncle Rick had more ammo somewhere in the house in case an actual motherfucker were to come and try some shit, because we heard him snoring, and a true Texan can't sleep unarmed.

A Case of Mistaken Indemnity

Drove through Dealey Plaza today, peering out the tinted rear window, drinking a Foster's oilcan. And to think that they could whisk away the cultural drain plug, just like that. At least he has left a legacy of the greatest songs ever—"I'm So Tired," "Across the Universe," "I'm Losing You," "Don't Let Me Down," etc. And poor Yoko in her pink pillbox hat, crawling horribly across the trunk.

Deepest Ellum

Sitting at the bar thumbing through the local weekly, nursing a beer while Motörhead soundchecks a Ronnie Spector song ("Be My Baby"), it is a good place to be. First one feels very thankful and important, and then a sweat comes on because you might actually suck after all. Sure your band rocks, but guess what? Not fucking really. Part of it is that, as anyone who has heard Motörhead in a big empty room would no doubt attest, the sheer volume blasts you back to the womb. Then they hit you with "We Are the Road Crew" or some shit and you're *done.*

Lemmy runs straight into a wall of custom Marshalls turned all the way up. He also takes his tea at four and sometime yesterday Mr. Kilmeister, irked, kyboshed the Nashville camp's tour flyer for being too racy. There are very few actual gentlemen or ladies in the world of hardest rock. Lemmy, above all, is a gentleman, and in this, is above all.

Lemmy summoned Theodoric after our set. Led over by one of the denim footmen, he was with great relief received with temperate praise and a shot of Jack, rather than with anything resembling disapproval—which would have been tantamount to a charge to hang it up, or wonder throughout our remaining career if we should have. We will rock at least one more day.

One More Day in Denver

Hotels are the answer to the question: shower, TV, bed. This one is a Bates job on the hill that overlooks the amusement park and the sports arena on the edge of town. Only one room because the rooms are large and the budget's shrinking. Bolted into town to get some food before everything closed, managing barely to get into a place purported to be the best tapas in Denver. They did serve small plates of things, but *no fue tapas* unless "tapas" means "hot wings" in Denver (note: it does). At a dollar or two each plate, we ordered the whole bar menu, comprising fourteen and a half things and totaling about twenty-two bucks. *Fucking excellent.* We were so excited that we ordered this food before we even asked about drinks—I don't have to say that that's pretty fucking excited. The place had an all right cup of clam chowder (not too thick, lots of clams, very little potato, reasonable with the bacon), and this carried us over into an order of notably uncontaminated clams on the half-shell. We're not alone in getting worked up over bits of food, because we're not the only band touring the late night of our fine nation. We eat nearly always in a nutritional black hole, on the treadmill of gas station coffee and vending machines, in big bright buildings where colors are flavors; we get pumped for a decent clam and downright *inspired* if it doesn't lay anybody out with dysentery. I sort of remember a blues bar after the meal, but at that point we had started drinking quite heavily, till around dawn. Late afternoon in the hotel, trying to extricate myself from the bedspread which had turned into an anaconda during the night. Have to have a piss, slept with my shoes on. Nobody's quite awake when somebody in morning voice creaks out, "Clams were *damn* fucking *good.*"

It's frequently difficult to relate to old friends when you're on the road—the grind is so insular, naturally resistant to outsiders. You're out more than a few weeks, and you're basically speaking in an alien dialect. Everybody's got a new name, inanimate objects are now living animals, and the interpersonal tension has, for better or worse, become oxygen. Non-nomadic persons don't know if you're talking about taking a shit or the weather. The tribe is for the tribe. A total stranger is an easier conversation; they don't know you from anyone and then it's on, or if it isn't, it doesn't matter.

Back from the packie in front of a sold-out theatre in Little D, not so much drunk from tequila as suddenly Aztec in pooling space cannon and colossal equilibrium damage. I rushed the front of the stage to crotch the P-bass and spray the audience dramatically with the imaginary fire of my loins, only to slam headfirst into my amp, which is at the back of the stage, near the pointing and laughing guy. The Denver crowd, like everything you need to revisit, is a very strange mix of love and hate, appreciation and disgust, beer, and women who look attractive from a distance. Certainly not bad, not bad at all.

Our Man in Wichita

Called the promoter for the Wichita show because Steve isn't feeling well. He's British. The Wichita guy, I mean. There was nothing in his voice that relayed an intention to treat our band as what we are—which is encouraging. He's doing shit at what I gather is a very sizeable place. I'm kind of picturing an indoor half-shell, like where the Pops play. He sounds like London society and that what the hell he's doing in Wichita is a fairly involved story. We were told to meet the promotions "team" at a bar situated on what Wichita has in the way of a promenade, and in the event that we arrived first to tell the bartender that we had been sent by so-and-so to drink everything and not pay, and that he'd be there after he "sorted out the Motörhead chaps." Knowing what is easy to know about Motörhead, I can say that "sorting out" Motörhead requires a heft of spirit most Earth-people lack—this guy either knows exactly what he's doing, or nothing at all.

Missing the Mark

The Loudest Band In The World requires—at least—a case of Maker's Mark, before they even get off the bus. Everyone with the Motörhead scene is a relaxed virtuoso when it comes to any procedural glitch but that one. If there's a hold-up with the bourbon, Motörhead village becomes a storm of running boots and madly jangling keys, slamming doors and distorted panic through the walkies. The mandate seems to be well respected nearly everywhere, with the exception of a bar in Wisconsin, where a fucking *idiot* promoter tried to substitute a half a case of Jim Beam, which he will *never* do again. Motörhead collected their booze and got back on the bus. We were kicking around in an alley. Phil Campbell came around with his fart machine, and the directions to the *new* venue.

Tit-Disneyland

Sauget, Ill.

Road sign: Sauget, Illinois. Pop 1200
The St. Louis arch is in view, until we pull into the club parking lot. The population of Sauget more than sextuples on the weekends because what you're looking at here are four interconnected strip clubs. The afternoon disappears: Phil, Lemmy, Mickey, Matt, Eugene, Steve, Mikey at the

bar: still life with *Motörhead* and The Unband drinking at the bar *all day long.*

Nashville Pussy is going off the tour. I don't know what happened. We took some pictures, they drove off, we moved up a slot.

I returned to the van in theatrical shock, waiting for phone calls and, casually, death.

We finished our leg of the Motörhead tour, wandering out of tit-Disneyland pregnant with hangovers. We're on good speed, tired permanently. The tour behind us will fall into the category of "successful," meaning that it was completed without loss of life or limb and fiscally irrelevant, aside from what we have in our pockets.

For the band, this could be a combined total of anywhere from twenty-five dollars all the way up to thirty dollars. Steve is going home to a respectable paycheck, but then again he's not so easily basking in the glories of "esoteric success" as we are—which is to say, silently watching the rain on the windshield and hoping something is next. When we get home, we are in grave danger of the classifieds and bumming drinks as if nothing had happened. That is, if the surrealistic European option doesn't pan out.

I passed out just over the border into Indiana and woke to an ethereal mist in the Smoky Mountains. Visibility's shit with fog. Too tired to look to my left to see whom, if anyone, is driving. It wasn't raining, but the wipers had a rhythm going. Stopping them would have interrupted the groove, broken the safety seal of exhaustion that keeps the focus on the road and protects us from flying off into the Whatever River. They don't tell you, but all this black comedy catches up to you on the drive home, even at

eighty miles per hour. The second you don't have a destination, the blob is on you. And thank God. The poison is
leaking out.

Woke finally on the West Side Highway. Outside another
Irish bar, Lenny gave us the news that we were to "get our
shit together" (whatever that means) and pack for a month.
(Same as for a week. There's really just one "pack.") Europe
is the best news possible. The tour and bus will be shared
with the Formidably Stoned Fu Manchu, sweetening the
pot, so to speak.

We'll be bagging sadly off the Grecian leg, Athens and
Thessa-something. Shit will start happening in London.

6

Eurotrashed with Fu Manchu

```
┌─────────────────────────────┐
│   Fu Manchu & The Unband    │
│      Oct.–Nov. 1999         │
└─────────────────────────────┘
```

Steam Room of the Damned

You can't see six inches in front of your face stepping into the Smokers' Lounge at JFK. Maybe the heaviest smoker in the world just went out the other end. I don't know if one can visually adjust to a thick toxic cloud, but shadows eventually take shape, fill in with colors, and people appear. We all must have done something terrible to be in here. There isn't even a fan. (I mean *come on*, point *taken*.) A German down the end snaps his newspaper, and the smoke billows as if he'd shaken out a cloud like a bed sheet. Everyone looks cracked and awful, as I'm sure I do.

High, Above the Pond

Somewhere over the Atlantic, October 1999

We had an early flight, so last night we were sensibly ordered to get sleep and "not be fucking idiots like you always fucking are, you fucking idiots." I crept into the bordello comfort of our manager's apartment on Third Street about seven-thirty with coke ground into my shirt-front and passed out two seconds later on the bearskin rug. Everyone else was wide-eyed in cabs on the way down to the emergency passport place with coke on their shirts. I can't be sure what happened down there, but I am certain it sucked impossibly. Waiting for government approval in the morning always does.

And then the Fucking Idiots are at cruising altitude noisily cocktailing for free. The stewardesses are not disappointing, sunny and pretty, extraordinary with the drinks and peanuts.

Puss has been to England, with a girl, in a past life as a collegiate Anglophile. Eugene speaks solid Italian; and Steve, dedicated provincial motherfucker that he is, hasn't been overseas even less than not at all, but flouts language barriers ably, fluent in the universal tongue of the wild barreling Yankee cowboy. There was initially some discussion about him not going and having Fu's tour manager double up, but in the end it was decided it would be best to have Steve—to keep an eye on our interests. And on, I suppose, our intake. It'd be unprofessional to burden someone outside the immediate family with the thankless dunce-wrangling job; we'd be outed as the bridge arsonists that we are.

I was in Ireland just prior to the last tour to visit my sister in Cork. Incredibly, there it seemed natural to get up at eight every morning. Among other inducements—something about the light—the pubs close at eleven. If you don't know anyone and you can't stand house music, there's little to do that isn't sleep. So, bed, then breakfast in the yellow row house at a bright table by the window; Irish bacon, a good newspaper, and a Guinness being loped unsteadily across the room by the doughy scone-matron. Then there is a pub to hit right away on the morning walk called the Stabbed Tourist or something. Jammed with drunks at 9:00 A.M., a good bar—very inexpensive, if a little stabby. Compare, the dawn drag at a Waffle House with its tedious fried things, the bitch waitress who doesn't like your "kind," your guts rumbling like Vesuvius, poring helplessly over pie charts in *USA Today*, pulling awkwardly off a warm Rolling Rock smuggled in a coat. And even the hotel bar is shut tight till noon. In Ireland, it's *better*.

When I was fourteen, there was a visit to Italy with the family, to tap the roots, including a side trip to Switzerland to see billboards advertise nutmeg-flavored soda by means of exposed breasts.

I saw my first glimpse of hard drugs from the window of a hotel in Venice. Two gentlemen were in the alley below, one with a fist of sweaty lira and the other in some kind of a cape, as I remember it. The whole transaction had a slow and sinless quality to it. It was a confounding thirty seconds.

I knew instantly that the little bindle the guy dipped his pinky into wasn't coke, because I had always figured that a cocaine deal would have an excellent and disaffected blonde, smoking in a black dress. I'm sure too it was the piety of the summer shadows, the stench of the canals, the Mediterranean breeze. I spent stretches of time over the next few days wondering what exactly that guy was getting for his money; and didn't put my finger on the core impression until the end of the long weekend there. I was standing with a crowd of tourists watching an old man blow glass. The most intense and intricate thing ever created bloomed in slow motion out of the end of his pipe. Ah, heroin.

Later that trip I lost the first of many hours to a blackout. I escaped the hotel leaving the standard pillow trick in my stead (this has worked suspiciously well throughout my life) and went wandering late in the streets. I met a kid at a café, a few years older and chainsmoking. He had noticed I was having trouble getting a beer and initiated a halting conversation. Our talk ended in mutually frantic *drinkydrinky* hand signaling, and then we were winding four flights of dim stucco towards, at least, a lot of garlic. I remember a crowded, smoky three-room apartment full of drunken Italians. They quickly handed me a jug of homemade wine, which I immediately shouldered and consumed. Later, I cut into an alley (I guess) off the piazza where the rain woke me up at 5:00 A.M. holding a heavy six-inch metal cross set with blue and red stones in one hand and the dirty shards of the wine jug in the other. The cross looked expensive, and the wine jug like evidence. I crawled back to the hotel, where sleep was foiled by a dripping faucet.

A few hours later I was steadying myself on a rope in Vatican City, battening down for a demonic projectile vomit. I was waiting, a nauseated agnostic, for an audience with the Pope. (When my father first mentioned this "audience" I initially pictured our family in the papal offices having whatever the Pope offers his guests—communion wafers and dip, a little wine.) It's ass in the morning, I have a spectacular hangover and here comes the Vicar of Christ. He's in the Popemobile, cutting through thousands and thousands of Catholics; his Holiness is waving and tossing out blessings like parade candy. Everyone's holding up little artifacts to be pope-d on, so I take out the cross and hold it up into the buckshot redemption as he comes by. My father asked where'd I get that, and echoes my suspicion that it's expensive (neither of us would have known). Doesn't matter, Dad, it's all good now.

I wore that debauched/beatified relic, all pound-plus of it around my neck for years, until the very first note of our very first show in Manhattan, at the Continental, when the string around my neck snapped. I saw the sacred doodad hang briefly in the gels before it went into the darkness at the front of the stage. It had been a weight belt through my adolescence of bounding in slow-motion across the sea floor, and then suddenly off, leaving me to pop to the surface of the Lower East Side like a choked fish in a cataclysmic environmental disaster. Looked for a while after the show, but . . . well, I hope whoever picked it up took special care—because that guy couldn't bless a sneeze now.

We're traveling miles up in the air by means of an incontestably flawed property; below us, three thousand miles of unthinkable watery doom—and you can't *smoke*? What happens if this thing starts going down? I'm going to spend the time I should be recanting going around in hysterics asking for a light.

But, I see it could be worse. I could be floating on a seat cushion in the middle of the Atlantic, not smoking.

There's a Bustle in Your Heathrow, and You Don't Know

We collected the baggage without hassle and got breakfast and beer. Looking over the *NME*, I'm on my third Winston in England, fucking pleased as hell. We have some time to kill before the bus arrives. Shed a few pounds then at the video arcade, shooting. "Pull!"

The bus, pulling into the underground parking horseshoe like a great whale beaching, hisses to a stop at our jumbled island of luggage. The plastic blowhole is barely a half a foot from the roof of the garage. It's a purple double-decker, and a tour manager comes out of it, clinking with back-stage crisis equipment. Alain is large, smiling, moustached, in a black fishing vest. I get the feeling he's putting on a little bit to assert some authority (he's probably been well prepped and we're not playing against type by being half in the bag already), but I do get the sense that he's all right, and that he knows exactly what he's doing at most times. A bouncing Welshman comes out next, and at first glance he is definitely one of the best men in the world. He's soft-spoken but gregarious, white hair and a dappled moustache. He introduces himself as Brian, and says something right away about boots that I didn't quite pick up, then helps with the bags, tossing anything musical into the lower cargo bins.

The bus is much better than expected, that is to say, not a fiction. The lower floor has two booths on either side, and airplane seating for two behind the far one, a kitch-enette and small storage area where one sways cross-eyed with a horrible late night snack peering blindly out a port-hole onto a dark moor. The "W.C." is adjacent, a nice place to not shit. The stairs bend a flight up, lit suitably enough for common drunkenness during the day by a long narrow window, aided by running lights for the more spectacular nighttime inebriations. To the right is a well-appointed lounge with a wraparound couch where WE DO NOT SMOKE ANYTHING BUT CIGARETTES, and to the left a crypt of thirteen bunks, some combination of which house the Mightily Dozing Fu Manchu. London rolls by, and well-behaved likenesses of The Unband look at it from the downstairs booths.

We stop at a music store for supplies: through an alley and an empty warehouse, out a metal door, then another, and up a flight of stairs to a cramped flute shop, obviously one that Alain frequents. I will note for the record that I had been "a pain in the ass" all week insisting that we stock up on incidentals before we left, being basically a tin-cup operation (whatever you think about getting "signed," traveling the world, fucking groupies, making records, etc. is true—but it's done on a subsistence budget until you're Bono or some fuck). I'm going: "The *Rolling Fucking Stones* had to *move* because they *couldn't afford England* . . . Sam Ash is having a liquidation sale . . . these are five cents online." Could not get the budget released because everyone assumed that the instant we had whatever money we'd be fanning it out in front of the first unsavory person we could find in an attempt to obtain drugs and things. This was an unqualified truth, and could have been monitored, to the tune of spare things and equipment not duct-taped.

The store has dusty flutes and brittle yellow sheet music, but also a number of necessities. Only—surprise—everything is heavily import-taxed and then hit with the *world-famous* UK exaction. Our entire equipment budget disappears in six minutes, leaving us accessorized for less than half the tour.

Steve's trying to call New York about money on Alain's clunky cell, which is the size of a WWII field phone, repeatedly fucking up the impregnable stream of numbers. We all stuck around for a minute or two, anticipating nothing, then vaporized one at a time to pod-up for naptime, in tandem with the Still Masked Fu Manchu.

The Garage,
London

Fu sold the place out to a good crowd. We played all right, but the bass, apart from needing some tonal attention, fucked off mid-set and so was unprofessionally switched out for the also fucked spare in a minute-plus of bumbling and humiliation. Consumed one vegetarian chicken sandwich from the "petrol" station, three something-something tall boys (warm), one-quarter bottle champagne, and uncounted vodka and Red Bulls with a small crew at a "speakeasy" in the East End.

We have a curfew, which will vary by city, but tonight is 1:00 A.M. The New York committee was *very* clear about abiding by this, though not as clear as Alain in those first few minutes on the bus: "We *will* fucking leave you behind, and that's *it*." We're missing somebody, so we've got time to run up the block to a fried chicken place inexplicably called "New York! Potato!"

During the trip to the Channel ferry, a card game got up and was smartly avoided by everyone but the four of us. Everyone probably can tell that our card games, without fail, deteriorate exponentially per minute till the final slope into a spirited Fifty-Two Pick-up. A descent from Hearts into spitting madness was observed numbly by Alain in the adjacent booth, doing the numbers. We had paper bags on our heads, singing something. You should see us at casinos.

Channel crossing was undertaken in the wee hours with the bus shut down in the belly of the ferry. I slept through it in my bunk, sweating with night terrors, fucking attacked with dreams about the price of cigarettes. "Ten dollars! Ten dollars! Fuck me! Ten dollars! Fuck me!" Couldn't find my smokes in the dark, drowsed back to a gas station. A girl was tossing bang-snaps (party poppers, or whatever; the paper teardrops with the twisted ends) near the pumps. I was inside buying cigs going, "Ten dollars! Fuck me!" when I noticed her. Burst out the door to stop her just as the pumps went up, and I bashed into the roof of the bunk. I could feel a huge egg emerging from my front head as the door downstairs opened noisily and someone said something, which was that we're in France.

On the way to Paris I rode with Brian in the cockpit. The windshield is floor to ceiling almost. Just after dawn and the countryside is soaked with froggy sentimentality, drear and rain. Brian's a European history buff, an expert really. We passed a place called Ruby Ridge (coincidence?), where the Germans first used gas, killing thirty-three Canadians (armed with cork pop-guns) "without firing a shot." He also mentioned that the monument to the attack involves numerous half-uniformed mannequins tossed around in the old trenches. Unfortunately, it was not a shit stop.

Went upstairs for more of this delicacy called "kip." At two in the afternoon, the bus was dark and empty. Over here, I always feel compelled and furthermore perfectly equipped to get up at ungodly hours, bolstered by random siestas. On this sleep schedule, apart from the 7:00 A.M. history lesson, I have seen almost no one, aside from Alain once, in the galley, bleary and silent with orange juice. Rolled feebly onto the street in my robe and socks, stretching, attempting to get my bearings, if they could be got (the door swiftly and quietly locking behind). The bus is parked precariously on a cobblestone island in the middle of an old busy street, sharing it not all that generously with a little magazine stand: Paris, obviously—coiffeur, banque, cake shop. Every inch attacked with ornament, a hustle of berets. I smell like a horse and need a smoke.

Must be some trick. No. No. No—it's locked? Wait, no.

Items locked inside the bus, aside from keys: cigarettes, itinerary with club information/cell numbers, shoes, shirt, sunglasses, French phrasebook, and money. Items on my person: none. Items required: one, cigarette. I start cutting a deal with God where if he lets me in just to grab my Winstons, I'll come back out *without* getting my shoes or *any-thing* and smoke in penitential silence at the boulangerie until the church bells call me to fucking Calvary if he wants. My face is reflected darkly in the tinted porthole of the door: Hey, kid. Fuck you.

Je Sui un Rock Star

First, I made a moronic attempt to charm the magazine stand woman into giving me some Silk Cuts. Unfortunately the French language intersects with mine at a point of only two words, and one is "shit." She watched my dirty bath-robe serenade, then laughed at me (not unpleasantly) and gave me what was left in her pack. That turned out to be a solid quarter pack, and I backed off bowing like a Chinese waiter. The options were as many as they were few, with nothing to lose in this remote French city. I sat on the ground and smoked out a plan. Trying to find the club was hopeless. Bumbling around in a bathrobe asking for direc-tions to the what, *chambre du Rock Star*? No. The touring party was probably spread all over the city, and even if I had money for fares of any type, I have zero knowledge of transportation here—a waste of my time, albeit as it is, worthless. So it was entirely a sightseeing expedition then as I began the trek up a steep street in Montmartre in my socks, smoking the Silk Cuts.

I stopped at a little chalkboard. Wine tasting.

I went, then, to taste.

One's "bearings" in any city—foreign, domestic, or alien—are got usually by finding a compassionate bar-tender, by not involving local authorities in anything, and with the help of the free local arts rag. Failing that, the kindness of strangers. Here I had found the paper, for what that was worth, and I was a free man about to receive free

wine. Shoeless but sorted, and in Paris. And so finally we
have it. It's a *good* thing I could never hold a job.

The Monsieur du Booze and his present company were
laughing the whole time. With or at me I don't know,
because I did not know at what I was laughing. I gave not
one single shit. They were pouring Chateau this and
Domain that, blind to expense.

"Eh. Yew are eeeh Rock Star? Ha. Ha. Ha."

"Oui. Je suis un *Rock* Star." Glug.

I emerged after the better part of an hour with red teeth.
Filled with vintages and new grammar, the American led
an invisible parade back to where, he thought, the bus was
parked. The parade was a success even though no one was,
unfortunately, walking a lobster on a leash.

Round the corner and . . . gone.

Wobbly triangulations based on the magazine stand and
the bank and the empty spot proved that, yes, the bus was
gone.

Fading, slugging half-dressed through the streets with the
lamps coming on, I ran out of ideas and began to sober up,
which is much worse even than running out of ideas. Eventually ran into a wandering Fu, of the Basically Responsible
Fu Manchu.

The club had been a vaudeville theater back when everything was more typically Parisian, that is, before television.
A good and thoroughly modern P.A. had been added since—
rolled in past a wary Victor Hugo, no doubt. Good crowd,
smelled of cheese. We played a show, and thereby a fine
time was had. I had learned, between becoming clothed and
soundchecked, to say "I am on the methadone program" in
French. In retrospect, I don't know why I thought this was
funny, except that it was in French, or how I could imagine
it would get a laugh from the crowd. They probably
thought it was just sad.

It was all very well received, and especially so following the AC/DC cover. The enduring miracle is that AC/DC covers are received well by all organisms advanced beyond a single cell, even played as badly as we play this one ("Rosie").

The buffet was deemed by the Cogently Epicurean Fu Manchu to be passable, but somewhat less than they might normally require. We—I anyway—have not yet developed a keen sense of catering tables, but it seemed to suffice in quantity at least, and the beer was Stella Artois, though it was not so cold. An impressive assortment of cheeses was removed to the bus by means of a guitar cable bag.

The showering was next, and would not go well.

Douche Rock Stars

I have had no problems with the French. All this business about Parisians being rude to Americans is bullshit. I was walking around like a fucking derelict all day, patently American, and was treated with charity and respect (so far as I could interpret), to the point of being wined expensively. Whereas in *any* American city I would have been locked up as a vagrant, and then been forced by circuitous legal disasters to become one. I will leave moderate elbow-room for the rampant accusations of non-bathing, but who's to talk; we *Rock Stars* smell like cattle right now, as I said— except for the girl. She smells nice. No, I have had no problem with the French. Until such time as I attempted to *douche* myself in the day room.

The operation goes in paired shifts. One *Rock Star* trolls four channels for something dubbed to watch while the other performs his basic ablutions, then they switch. After a reasonable duration, the next pair of hygiene seekers calls up to the room and is traded off the key. I was the last man, unpaired. I toddled into the lobby of the hotel, more than mildly discomposed. And though my condition was derived paying exclusively French taxes, the night monsieur will not buzz me through the half gate. He does not believe that *je suis un Rock Star,* and he would prefer if I left *le Hotel.*

No! Intoxi-can!

And now, ladies and gentlemen, some impressionism. *Falling terribly over the gate. Someone else. Someone else over the counter. The jugular of a caustic Frenchman. A hidden parlor. Flying marble chess pieces. A shaving kit swung like a mace. A plant joust. A slip in the shower.* Paris is a long day.

We left the City of Fights late, because of bathing and policemen. But the rush had ceased to matter; the Lisbon show all accounted wasn't worth it and was scrapped by cellphone. The plan had been to fly everybody non-commercially, rent things, etc. Then somebody returned that page of the itinerary to the Crazy Talk pile, and Portugal was left to the Portuguese, leaving us a free day.

After everyone had put themselves in their little overnight delivery slots, partly to avoid drinking *both* of the '88 du Papes myself, I went up and rode with Brian. He was twinkling about the regrettable necessity of the Allied attack on the French fleet at Oran. I suspect, knowing Brian, that this is a kindly gesture towards my unfortunate affair at the hotel. I've learned more about the Third Republic at Vichy in the past two days than would have been possible in any other context than this—warm from narcotic mints and Châteauneuf du Pape, Europe stretching out for a month in every direction. After a few hours, we pulled over in a lot off the highway and drank whiskey. Good whiskey that Brian keeps in his bunk for sipping after the drives, in glasses that look dollish in his hands. Napoleonic wars tonight, outside the window was McDonald's, lit for a prison break.

Having a hard-on for the South of France, affiliated with having read *Up and Down With the Rolling Stones* years ago, I went on probably too long in a sap fantasy about riding horses through the Mediterranean shallows and crashing a Bentley. Brian went to get a few hours of fine imported kip and get us well into Spain so we can kick around. Everybody else has been sleeping since three bottles of wine into the drive. Now I go bed.

Attack of the Fifty-Foot Woman

San Sebastian, Spain
10/26/99

Woke very late, 4:30 P.M. The door of the bus opened onto a concrete boardwalk being strolled by a good many people.

Back in Massachusetts, there's a 50-foot Virgin Mary leveling a beam of bionic guilt across Revere Beach, where Jimmy McClue is currently digging in red tide muck and ranting about his *fuken* alimony.

Here, presiding from the hilltop to the left, is another towering statue of the Blessed Mother, ready to battle Mothra. The far railing overlooks a drop to the beach. Out straight is a pitching blanket of whitecaps, infinite till Corsica.

After freshening up, we attend directly to the sidewalk bar and order Stellas until we tire of drinking them, long after everyone else around. Steve joined us for a bit, but is taking a personal day. The bank card is consumed at primitive ATM, so we proceed with an untried card to a basement *restaurante*, pile the table with fish and sangria, and dig in with crossed fingers. The card goes through, even un-activated, and so we take a photo of ourselves with the waiter.

The streets had become deserted during the time we were eating, which we only then noticed had been for over three hours. The restaurant's posted hours indicated that they had been closed for two of those. Dinner had been quite fucking superb, and we had a good buzz going; we became mildly frantic nonetheless, now aware that we had missed the winestore. There was nothing left on the bus. So we hunt.

Roaming the streets, we met up with some architecture students. Two Italians and a Portuguese, all *borracho*. They took us to a bar with no mixers for the vodka, but the music was AC/DC, Aerosmith, and Stones. A Moroccan kid had some hash, and, eventually, a little coke (not terrible). Steve was fetched then. A Brit showed up with more blow (terrible, but whatever). Usual mindless chatter ensues—a linguistic massacre. Closing time all that was left was a pig-pile of singing idiots. We bought a couple bottles of generously discounted unlabeled booze off the bartender and moved toward the bus swaying like movie drunks before they get rolled by the wolfman. Steve, rested from his personal day, became inspired and went running around on the beach screaming with his pants down for a long, long time—as in looking at your watch long. As in fuck it, let's just drink this right here long.

Nowhere on the beach could we hide from the giant Virgin and her disapproval, so we went for cards on the bus. More singing. Brian thought funny. Alain not. He's been awakened. Not *too* sure about his level of amusement with us on the whole. Is dumbstruck and bug-eyed on the stairs good or bad? We don't know.

Which is why, I suppose, we are here in the first place.

Spanish Speaking Gentlemen

Barcelona
10/28/99

Soundcheck, eat some cheese. The runner comes wanting to know if there's anything we need. Silently checking with one another, weighing certain risks. One of us says cocaine.

"Okay. No problem. How much you want?" says the guy who is called Enrique.

"Enough."

"I take care. One hour."

Very nice meal at a small restaurant near the club, jugs of wine, sardines. Wandered around some tourist area for a while.

Good crowd, very, and not due exclusively to the endless hail of drugs arcing to the stage all night for both bands. And Enrique reported back, profusely. Gak-ed to the tits riding out of Bahr-theh-lownah, the four of us plowed through nearly a case of wine, with a little help from the Excruciatingly Hilarious Bob and Brad from the Increasingly Endearing Fu Manchu.

Fucking Off in the Camargue

Les Saintes-Maries-de-la-Mer
Remembered: drooling on to Brian about riding horses
on the beach in the South of France.

Day off. A good percentage of the time we—at least I—
don't know where we are until I open the bus door. This
morning was one of those, but instantly registering as a
beautiful trick. The ocean was visible from the doorstep,
the view blocked only by a sign that said

Chevaux→

This was an unprecedented act of luxury, perpetrated by
the best guy ever, an understated Welsh bus pilot.

The horses were a bit riled from an earlier thunderstorm,
and were unstill while a wraithlike wine-soldier from Nar-
bonne attempted to attach primitive saddles to them. Six of
us led by the wine-soldier rode through town, then onto
the beach. Some fat German tourists who had couponed
onto our party held up the caravan repeatedly, honking
with complaints from fifty yards *beck*. The guide let us
(myself and Twiggy the sound girl) ride ahead after voicing
frustration with the Germans and assuring him we knew
what we were doing. We popped ahead a bit in a casual trot,
the horses stopping to eat sea grass here and there. My
steed started waking up a bit in the rapidly cooling air, and
would no longer maintain less than a full trot, taking it
alternately to waves and dunes. I was alone way up the
beach with a bruised tailbone already when he woke up
fully and revealed himself to be an equine Rolls driven by
Keith Moon—he fucking *bolted*. This was well beyond my
YMCA camp experience, nothing to do but hang on. The
wine-soldier was whooping with glee, shouting some Dopp-
lering instruction as we barreled past him, a hoof storm

now going in the other direction. The horse was looking for a plate-glass window to crash through, so as to cause spectacular damage to a tea party, and be congratulated by other horses. I was doubtful he would find this soon, as he was heading directly out to sea. I was locked onto the horse's neck, a drunk with a third-degree rope-burn, ecstatic with fear. He turned around and headed back to shore when the waterline moved far enough up his neck. Soaked and freezing, and in mortal danger, ripping down the Côte d'Azur, and the sun going down like it'd been shot.

The horse didn't stop for almost an hour. Once or twice he slowed almost to a stop, but as soon as I made a move to dismount, he'd go rocketing off again. Here he would add a trip through some thorns to make up lost time. When he did stop, we were hell and gone from anything recognizable. He ate some grass and snorted around looking for pills. There was really only one road, thankfully, which would preferably be walked so that the road may get its kicks in too. I would not be troubled by additional injury since I had lost all feeling below the ribcage (also possibly collapsed) before we even got to the place with the screaming farmer. The horse, suddenly personable and obedient, let me down to shamble with destroyed vitals towards town. He, not being in ideal condition to begin with, was sapped, his gray tongue lolling out his mouth like an old steak, narcotically clomping through dark streets. Everyone had long since gone to fish restaurants.

Back at the non-AAA certified stable, our man was on a wicker thing snoring ferociously in a wine coma. He opened one eye as I handed him the rope connected to the horse. He was wasted and furthermore didn't give a shit. He departed again to his gurgling oblivion with the rope in his hand, leaving the horse just enough slack to get to the trough, which may or may not have contained regular water.

Treachery and Fog

The bus has come to rest somewhere. The ebbing of the engine woke me. Any change in the rhythm of anything stirs me nowadays. Out the window on the stairs, it's pitch black, as if we're inside something. No echo though. Peering out the open door provides no clarity other than a sense of wide space and the smell of wet. Didn't try all that hard to go back to sleep, instead began rooting around for liquor, which I found handily. Killing some time deciphering the cartoons in a French magazine when Steve came down the stairs, Greg Allman on a medium day, and sat down. When the bottle was gone and we had recaptioned all the comics, the sun came up.

I sincerely doubt there has been a fog this thick since the Triassic period—literally unbelievable. The landscape is no less mysterious than in the pitch night, and must be found out. So we put on things, drunkenly shushing each other, grabbed one of the pre-rolled hash cigarettes from the tin, and went in morning voices onto the moonscape. A lump in my sock became immediately uncomfortable. Stepped out of the bus, fog sacks over our heads, escorted blindly off into Italy by Calvados.

The walking was hugely difficult; the mud grabbed at our knees. I don't know how far we went, we might have been walking in heavy, labored circles. The return route was even more elusive and monstrous after the hash, and were it not that the hum of the bus generator was the *only* sound, we'd still be there. (Little Italian children would entreat their parents hysterically to leave baskets of liquor on the stoop to appease the Vanished Americans hunting in the night forever for the Purple Bus.) My feet were killing me when we got back. Upon applying the necessary violence to remove my shoe (unknowingly spattering the vicinity with great quantities of muck), a small fist of hash popped out, landing . . . somewhere.

The remaining adventure has been pieced together crudely. I'm sure the effort to locate the hash was some-what less than discreet. By way of example, let's take a quick trip back home. Say we've been staying with a woman a little over a week too long. Perception: "What, last night? I went out to the supermarket, got in about midnight, silently put the eggs in the fridge, got into bed, gave you a gentle little peck and fell asleep, slept like a rock." Reality: after announcing a quick trip to the super-market and the video store, you stop at a suddenly remem-bered art opening for a sec and have fifteen glasses of wine, then a Mind Eraser, a Jaeger and two somethings at the next place, then, after being sailed to the pavement outside a topless crack-house where you smoked a joint with *Yolanda*, you go and slug half a bottle of Absolut in some-one's kitchen at four in the morning—never, by the way, having been *near* anywhere with groceries or movies unless you count baking soda and total retinal disconnect. Then you "creep" back to the woman's apartment, charley horse on the coffee table breaking an heirloom vase, topple an end table, root around blindly for liquor, slamming kitchen cabinets and swearing audibly, wake up the roommate and torture her with incoherent nonsense until she goes in her room and locates the vermouth from the Derby party six months ago which you snatch, tumbling with it into the right room (this time) to promptly dump it all over your benefactress whatsername's computer, then crashing to the bed, rocking it heavily spilling change everywhere while trying to wrench your pants over your shoes, just before—ignoring a total inability to perform—pouncing on her like a coyote and almost breaking her nose. Then, ripping the covers off her, you commence tossing and snorting like a beast until it's time to throw up all day. Meanwhile, no one is having eggs, anywhere, or watching the movie about e-mails.

So the manner by which I found the drugs was probably not as subtle as I imagined it to be. Out of courtesy, I go and smoke on the roof (denting it and shaking the whole bus).

The sun is slowly illuminating a vast patch of northern Italian country at the foot of the Alps. Satisfied with the view from atop the bus, I was finally set to retire. And so I yanked open the vent above the lounge, dislodging (though not permanently) numerous safety features in the process, and tried to slip through it quietly—instead plunging to the table like a Christmas mailbag, my limp body being discovered there by a dismayed Welshman. "Yu've git sum werk ta do this merning, Mikey," he said with calculated calm.

I'm fucked under the table with a smashed, burned-up piece of fruit in my hand. Evidently I had been smoking the hash from an apple*. Tried my best to make good, and thank God Brian is, literally, the best man in the world, but if *he's* pissed . . . thank God no one . . . the bus in that condition . . . it hurts to speculate, or move.

Brian told me the vacuum was in the boot. Okay. (I have no idea what he's talking about. The what?) The boot. Okay. Looking under things in the galley. "*No*, mate. In the *boot*." Oh, right. Sorry. (So fucking confused.) He doesn't stop me as I go out the door, so I figure I'm getting warmer. I'm walking around the bus trying . . . the *boot*? My shoe comes off in the mud. I can't get it out. I'm hopping and working at it as Brian comes around.

"Ya doon't know whet the boot is do ya, Mikey?"

"Um. Yes, I do. Or, actually . . . no. I didn't want to bother you."

Laughing, he opened up a cargo door to reveal a few guitars belonging to the Deftly Innocent Fu Manchu, and the wet vac. He thought it all very funny, especially with the

---

*Fruit, apples, bananas, pears—anything non-citrus, can be easily (and even ceremoniously) ejected from the lounge hatch ten miles before borders, undetected. In a real emergency the paraphernalia can be eaten, but this is unpleasant and almost never happens.

hopeless shoe. I guess it was, but for the guilt. Then again, that's the Pope's fault, not mine. I cleaned the shit out of the bus with the help of some of that Barcelona speed that makes you go deaf.

Brian ribbed me later at the buffet about going on like he was really that pissed (says he wasn't much at all, in which case he got me), and adds the only serious note by saying he doesn't want to see anybody get hurt, plus a little information related to the British insurance industry.

That was *almost* the last time I got stoned on the roof of the bus.

Pezzos di Stonatos

(Riffs of the Stoned Ones)

The building we are to *rock* is a freestanding pea green structure, even more isolated in the *compagna* than previously envisioned. The poster by the entrance read: "Not unlike Kyuss. Rock made by American *Stoners.*" This is, as everybody's grandmother says, much funnier in the Italian.

Our host here could not be more pleased to receive his guests. Babbo goes around the room extending two-handed shakes, beaming. He proudly introduces his sons all around and details the items on the endless dressing room antipasto. Then he claps his hands and rubs them briskly a few times, asking if there's anything more we need before he leaves us to our private ("stoner") world. We're quite happy and so he ushers the sons out of the dressing room quickly and closes the door smiling, having provided the most beer yet.

After lolling around the dressing room with prosciutto and Stellas for a time, one of the sons, Luca, knocks on the door to see if anyone would like to go for a spin around town. There's a town? Then yes, The Unband would like to see it. Luca, dark and casually Versace, loads us into his brand new eighteen-cylinder sports car, peels out onto the tree-lined road, and launches into conversational English. He points out the particulars of the landscape and the nightlife (girls), asking polite questions about the tour (girls), and so forth. After thirty minutes or so, we're parking semilegally on the *strada principale*.

I have yet to see Biella on a map other than a regional one I saw in a shop window here. This is strange because it's an ample town of loud crowded streets and looming architectures. Had drinks in a small bar with several of our guide's friends, one American, and formulated a post-show plan of unspecified druggishness. Doing okay with the language by now—not great, but have surpassed "please," "thank you," and "my friend is addicted to acid." Bought some postcards and some lickerish for my father.

Backstage at the club, Babbo is Italianly supervising the construction of a new drum riser, and has his people (multiplying hourly) generally occupied around the stage in an opening night crunch of hammers and ropes. We require no extra carpentry or anything we insist, and get back to alcoholic reclusion in *la camera di prosciutto*. Luca pops his head in, we've been drinking and stringing for an hour or so. "My father would like to know if it's no trouble to introduce you to the neighbors." The neighbors, an older couple, no English, a presence like a moveable hearth. They had walked a mile to see the commotion, and delivered homemade wine to stash on the bus for use at some point in the future—one might predict to add bucolic civility to a disgusting act.

After soundcheck, Babbo set up a kit kitchen on the back bar. He and the sons began cooking while his wife stocked the tables with sweet liquors and fresh bread. The spread is family style—plenty for bands, crew, and Babbo's people. Babbo-lonia is now expansive with cousins and twinkling grandmothers, uncontainable at any one table, barely accommodated by three. The food is incredible. There's lamb with gravy, whole fresh trout, sausages, stufato, and some fowl—a woodcock or something—in sauce. Babbo's smiling and singing and stirring polenta. There's roasted artichoke, hand-rolled fontina gnocchi and another more Americanized and vegetarian pasta dish just in case, a massive salad, stracciatella (a Babbo specialty) . . . and of course a brilliant coffee situation.

The evening's rock, almost an afterthought by this time, is excellent. Did realize quite suddenly on stage that as universal as the throwing of goats is, in Italy if you do it with your hand anything like level, you are cursing someone by dooming their lover to be unfaithful. Mental note. The after-show bit took place in a huge nightclub playing mostly American Rock, intermittently lifted by the brilliant Italian version. A live band came and played at some point. After their set (quite good) Luca enthusiastically brought us over to meet them, adding a Masonic nod when he introduced the Manager. A few minutes later, I'm in the passenger seat of the Manager's sports car which he did not earn "managing" any bands.

He asks if I like classical music, and slips in a CD, turning up (I shit you not) "The Ride of the Valkyries," and tears off into the streets densely roamed by the night-populace. People have to jump clear of the hood each time he glances down to count out bags from his pocket. He explains the social position of each local he doesn't accidentally kill. If this was his typical drug-dealing tactic, well, it was madness, and he was enjoying it immensely, as was

I (I'll just tell the *policia* I was hitchhiking). When we have screeched back into the club lot and sent a parking cone flying and I'm thanking him (a bit shakily) for the whole thing, thrusting miniature Ziplocs into my pocket, with the door handle primed, he says—humbly and sincerely—that he must ask me a very important question. "Of course," I say with only minor trepidation. In his best English yet, he says carefully, "You are born an American, *si*?"

"Yes."

"Okay, my friend. Then if you would, my friend, tell me something."

"Sure."

"Tell me, *why* would you eat the salad *first*?"

Gimme Indie Rock, and Some Chips

Milan
Halloween

They definitely don't have Halloween over here, thank God. Last thing I need is people in masks and giant arachnids everywhere.

The *Italian* promoter, from *Italy*, offered up a catering table with exactly this:

1. Paper plate w/chips
2. Paper plate w/*chopped hot dog*
3. No "3"

Do they even *have* hot dogs in Italy? Where the fuck did he *get* hot dogs? And anyway, there isn't enough of that even.

Our rather "disappointed" scoutmaster got physical, lightly, reasonably, and then apologized for over-reacting. But it was not enough for Oscar di Mayer, who said the worst thing he *possibly* could have, and soon the atrium was filled with flying Englishmen and shouting Italians. Then *polizie*.

We were deathly bored by attacks from the constabulary

I felt a little for the guy, but only because of something he said in a conversation earlier, over warm Turk sodas. He asked how we were "doing," meaning girls. Before we could say anything (and he did not know where we were from):

"In Meelan, even *See-bah-doo* get girls."

Well, we ought to be fine, then. Thank you. Please pass the nothing.

Having Been to the Moon, I Say Keep It

Zurich, 2 November

It's Zurich for women.

Or it would be, were it not for *you*, my little bougainvillea, my little chook. You know *that*. Yes, of course. Hey, you know, would you mind making me another one of these? Yeah, it's downstairs, in the noisy thing. Yes, refrigerator. Thanks.

You ever been to Zurich? Well, let me tell you, they're—What? No, no, I don't need new ice. Thanks. Nooo. *You* are. No, thank *you.*

In Zurich, they're coming out of the subways. They're going into the subways. They're buying newspapers, coffees, talking on cell-phones, freshening up. They're parachuting into the square, they're hauling up out of manholes, snipping through the wire, lifting their *dire* gams over the back walls. Commandeering shops, rappelling down the building sides, buzz-bombing, snorkeling up through tub drains, fusillading the *autostrade. It's a blitz.* It's Night of the Living Bombshells.

Frankfurt

Nov. 3?

Arrived early in a suburban neighborhood. Stopped in at a coffee stand. I've got a touch of German going, but as soon as I began to order, the woman, shocked, slammed down a gate. I checked the book a while ago, and I think I may have asked for coffee with soap in it. Which might have made sense actually—I looked like shit.

No idea where I was going really, except towards the enormous bank building. Estimably very distant, but I thought I might find some camera batteries near it, which is to say I'm just wandering. I don't know . . . what the fuck do *you* do in suburban Frankfurt at 7:00 A.M.? Passing through an industrial area, I was tailed from across the street by a loping character who was taking unjustified interest in my progress. I glanced at him, gave a little wave which he obviously mistook for some kind of gang sign. He crossed the street, dodging whipping cars. He was an Armenian from Munich (it turned out), dressed as if he had only gotten half the memo from Tommy Boy. "Vaas ahhp, yo?"

"Nein?" I guess. What the fuck is this now?

"Yo, you half ze bang?"

Bang? Bang. . . . bang . . . *bhang,* maybe? This being warm milk with THC, is an odd thing to assume a strolling American early-riser to be carrying, and though he could not have assumed I was anything other than that, I can't think what else he might mean. So I crook an elbow and he nods. He seriously thinks I'm carrying a cannabis smoothie somewhere on my person.

"Yo, less check it."

I kept walking, not really sure what was happening. It occurred to me that homey might take it upon himself to try and roll me. His take would be a couple marks, a cheap Swiss Army knife, and a partially completed list of acknowledgments for our record insert with a tiny ball of hash contained in a folded corner.

"Yo. Lemme rhyme aht choo van time yo."

This began an hour or so of listening to rhymes, most of which were *not.* Then things started getting a bit strange. Everything he said edged eventually toward a very sudden drop into vengeful world-grief. This was shortly after we had finished off all the hash. He wasn't getting violent, not yet, but it was time to lose him before he did, and even without the creeping psychosis, the guy *could not* stop rapping. I was beginning to realize just how unmanageably high I was, now that I was having some concerns.

I imagined I could count on the fact that the Armenian wouldn't notice that I was doubling back because he was intensifying, rapping directly onto my face, his head halfway through a Linda Blair twist. I was trying not to look at him and leaving a mental trail of breadcrumbs (immediately pecked away by mental birds). I'm going to wander through these gardens for *hours*. I'm going to be left behind, or worse yet, neither of those things, but rather be responsible for siccing this crazy on everyone else when I go back for soundcheck. No. No soundcheck, if it comes to that. After some elaborate convincing, I went for a piss without his company. The small central pigeon feeding area was reasonable with trees, and as soon as I was in them I made my way towards one of the garden plots. I could still see him through the trees, bouncing like a chicken. I hopped over a fence and jammed myself into the space between two tool sheds. I was covered but aware that I may have invited on myself a new trouble, being that I just mashed someone's prize zinnias and now I could be trapped in here from either side. That was only a possibility. Immediately, though, I was high enough to think there were *insects* getting on me, probably a hail of arachnids.

When I hit the raw pavement I turned, exhausted, jogging slowly backwards, saw just the empty street, and stopped to lean on a parked car. Not *sure* if all that was necessary.

Liverpool, We Have a Problem

Hamburg, 2:30 A.M.

Matt, Steve, and I disembarked the instant Brian pulled the break. (Eugene also, but a promotions girl stuffed him into one of those antiquated pneumatic message tubes. Whoosh.) We were approached just as quickly by respectable-looking strangers (well, strangers) who were anxious to give us advice on the manner and means by which to procure the attentions of the finest ladies of the Reeperbahn. The corner of the two most streetwalked streets in Hamburg is occupied by none other than a McDonald's. The cabbie observed us with a friendly wink in the rearview when we told him to take us there.

There are some very attractive girls strolling the Reeperbahn. They look like a dispersing rap audition, all wearing the same brand new puffy white ski coat. I feel more comfortable in red-light districts when it's time to do some professional drinking. I will have very little work to do to be entertained, and therefore tend to get into *less* trouble than at the Embassy Suites anywhere, and here it's affordable. We chose an empty bar on a populated corner because we could hear "Miss You" coming out of it.

Two women behind the bar. They were maybe twenty years apart and gave the impression of being an unrelated mother and daughter. They both looked exhausted and foolproof. The older one addressed us as soon as we entered, her hand going under the counter.

"Zis is not a place for za *Breeteesh*."

"Fuck the British," said the very wise Mr. Steve Sanderson, *around* whom the question was directed.

"You are American zen?"

American Zen.

"Goodt. Sit."

A shadow was croaking in the far corner, and a couple sat at a table at the far wall. Empty otherwise. We took seats midway along and ordered. The Frau pulled the pourer off each bottle, and filled our glasses. I stared at mine. I had forgotten what a full glass of liquor looked like outside of the bus.

"Yoo are vat khind uf *rohk* bahnd." It wasn't really a question. She said "rock" beautifully.

"We're a baseball team." Steve says this every time. It's fairly perfect—whatever it's supposed to do, it works.

The Frau looked at her partner, who exhaled toward the ceiling.

"Beyhzbahl has *nein.*"

We were three each, then. They seemed to enjoy this, by which I mean they laughed, where ten seconds ago you would have thought them incapable. "Ohh. I see you are looking fuhr guhrlz. Zeah ah no gurhls in zis place." In fact, there was a gentleman being violently fellated on the pinball machine in the back, a noise that had become impossible to avoid. The Frau waved it off.

"Vat mewsic du you play?" The younger woman was crushing out her cigarette. She had taken some time to put herself together tonight, probably not unusual. She has more hope than her colleague.

"Yah. Vat mewsic."

Hard Rock.

"Ech," observed the Frau.

"She doesn't like it. She likes bluegrass. But I like eet. I like very loud mewsic, too. Vahn Halen." This woman was . . . interesting, in a sort of I'm leaving tomorrow kind of way. It was not hard to have a mental picture of a brilliant situation on the bus, the Reliably Snoozing Fu Manchu awoken (again) in their berths trying to imagine two forty-year-old Transylvanian alcoholics. It was a nice picture, but in another way, not really.

"Yah. Ze bluegrass is goodt. I can blay szome. A leetle."

"She iss very tahlentedt fuhr ze bahnjoe."

The door opened and a *British Rock Band* let itself in noisily. British Rock Bands seem to make certain German barfraus want to kill them with a shotgun. I don't know why. Some of my best friends are British Rock Bands—but these women were dead set. Neither moved to serve them.

"Zeah iss nahsing fuhr you heere." The Frau was not looking at them.

The drummer was instantly indignant. The guitar player was putting money in the jukebox.

"Zayy . . . pleeez."

They did, ineffectively.

"*Nein*. Get out."

The British Rock Band was looking at us as the Frau approached them, getting the most out of her cigarette. "If you do not get out I vill zshoot you."

The British Rock Band should have taken the hint. They did not. From our vantage, the shotgun butt was just visible. The guitar player protested, not entirely without tact and legs to stand on, that he has invested in the jukebox, and therefore ought to be served. She reluctantly brought glasses to them, but only filled the pints three-quarters up and charged them double or so. They took it for the moment.

The conversation turned here and there, Steve left, the Brits were barely tended. The Frau opined on our place of origin. "Maszachewsitts. Za police in Bahstuhn are ze raszist." She became vocal on the topic of ze barbaric American Police with their use of handcuffs. At one point she said (a little hopefully) to Matt, "Yoo prahbablee like zeez hahndcuffs," and the Fräulein took to this. "Yah! I szink so!" The Brits, growing increasingly ornery, were about to get it. I went to the bathroom while Matt wrote down the show information for the Fräulein. The Fellatrix was in the men's room with her lesser half. They were in oblivion, rubbing each other in puffy white ski jackets. He still held a spike. She looked bad, but he looked much worse. A mild commotion began and subsided as I walked out. I returned to my seat. Matt was gone and so was the British Rock Band, and the Frau was snapping something into place under the bar. The other woman was exhaling and mumbling something. Matt emerged from the other toilet and returned, both of us to fresh drinks.

"No more British?"

The Frau's mood had improved. "Zat iss dah last time zey vill come to zis place."

I asked her what it was about British Rock Bands that made her so . . .

"Szey assoom too much." Said the Frau.

"Zey cahm to Hahmbourg and zey szink zey are za Beetlesz. But zey are *not* za Beetlesz." Said the Fräulein.

After seven or eight more drinks, a most amazing thing happens. Matthew Pierce, shit-housed on the Rheperbahn at 2:00 A.M., after ignoring shotguns and junkies with their pants down, whores at the window like moths, and everything else, looks down into a dirty shot glass of Courvoisier and says there is a bug in his drink.

The Frau answers absolutely. "Goodt. Now yoo have szumsing to eat too."

Blue Balls on the Baltic

Rostock-Trelleborg ferry

I had never tasted sea air like Baltic sea air. I had never seen a show where gorillas spoke in Dutch. I had never approached a fjord, let alone seen one through a porthole in a playroom on the main deck of a ship. And I have never slept so well as I did passing out cold in a tub of soft blue plastic balls on a nearly deserted ferry to Sweden.

7

Anthrax's Plodding Sausage Party

**Anthrax, Fu Manchu
& The Unband
U.S. Tour Jan. 2000–Feb. 2000**

Are We Not Metal?

Blaaaaaat....... Blaaaaaaat......... Blaaaaaaat......
    "*Fucking... ow.... fu.... shit..... mmph....
Hello?.... Ah... Hey, how's it uh... go? -Ing....
man.... No no no, I'm awake, just a little... um, I have
a uh... something with my uh... uh... thing... never
mind... what's?......... Really? Uh-huh... I see...
Riiiight..... Yes. Yes of course, but... who?......
What?... Those people are gonna fucking hate us... no,
suh...... it just doesn't make...... yeah, well, let me
put it this way. What if you came to work every day and
Sheila from marketing kicked you in the nuts just for
showing up? I mean...... fuck...... Uh-huh... yes....
I'm listening.......... uh-huh... okay, okay......
mmmmmm...... for every show? Is that guaranteed? Are
you absofuckinglootly sure?... Well, what KIND of potato
chips?*

The Anthrax tour started off reasonably enough with two shows in New York, fairly insane shows, but really a dry run for Jersey, spiritual home of Metal. They should put something on the license plates in New Jersey: Wunt Dunt Dunt.

Yeah, well we probably should not be on another tour like this, but being on the big metal bill in the metal capital is love. Metal's got the jump on everything where it's appreciated, dedication in epic numbers. Black T-shirts, hair, beer, leather, the line snakes for blocks. As a betting man, my six remaining dollars are on the Army of Darkness in Old Bridge, Marlboros hanging off their lips, air drumming in a deep Jersey sunset.

Drinking in the van in the parking lot, fiddling with the TV antenna, we are very much not working on our chops. Already we're pressed for time and everything else, so all this business with the shredding of the notes is counterproductive for us. We only have space for—*one, two, three*—six chords in total. Seven if you count hitting all the open strings at once. So we milk them a bit. So what. Cows live a long time, and they're mostly idle. Besides, it'd be foolish for us to write anything we can't play drunk, and this rules out chords other than A, and not the minor one, either. Nope, we are not real Metal, whatever nut-busting Sheila from marketing says.

Any hardcore Anthrax fan is going to call bullshit on us every night this month, though we have never promised him anything, least of all "chops" or a soundtrack to his landlord murder fantasy. But, hey, you go to your job every day (well, you know what I mean) and we go to ours, which is the same as a regular job but with more drinks and so forth. And being so employed, we will dutifully embark another series of hundred-hour drives and involuntary hunger strikes for our bread and butter: thirty minutes of being pummeled by projectile debris and heaps of derision, most of which we take *straight* to the bank, and the rest we donate to various charitable organizations. Then we reward ourselves with eating a carrot from the thrice-dumped deli tray, flicking the ashes out of the dip, and sitting back and waiting for our next glories.

The thing to do is go out and play and hope that by the time anybody starts throwing full beers at the stage we're in the filthy van halfway to the next city, hopping over embankments and little river bridges with the chick from catering slurring that the seatbelt is poking her and her hot friend has to throw up again. Sometimes, it just doesn't feel like work at all.

They were called DAMAGER. According to their bass player, they were all descendants of Thor, who, it turns out, had some part of his ancestry relocated or maybe exiled from the sky (unclear) to a Massachusetts suburb with real estate investment possibilities and a better school system.

Then, when the night goes away like it always does and it's tomorrow, one guy is transported magically to a Copy Cat at the mall where his daily reaming by the junior manager is already in progress, one guy pops awake in the middle of a music store where he is already blazing through Wagnerian scales at jet volume while housewives who "don't know shit" buy recorder music, and one guy is beamed into his Masturbation Chair in a furnished basement where *Krull* is playing on a squeaky Betamax, again. This will all change when they force Metallica and everyone into early retirement by brutally out-rocking them—it's just a waiting game.

Shows took place at the Congregational Church. Next week, *next week* in the donut room, where most usually parents shame and press their children into the crab claws of the knitting-ladies, in the donut room, it's all Damager—live, *killing*. DAMAGER! Plus Special Guests.

Our men Damager rolled up with an eighteen-wheeler and six guys just to unload their ninety-nine-piece drum kit. They might have been off to play the Garden. But it was not easy for Damager. Between the demands of the roadies, the new pyro requirements, the clumsy removal of the Rector's portrait, the now scratched linoleum, and the hiding of the dented percolator and the broken card table which got sat on by Ox the Giant Evil Puppet Operator, and add the gathering reality that no one is coming to the show—well, the situation is unmanageable and snow-balling, and it's mayhem in the donut room. There's a giant mess of drum hardware and enormous amplifiers and upside down crosses and people dropping shit. Then there's the puppet, which I have no idea what the fuck it was besides more or less conventionally "evil."

Now here comes The Unband with short hair and thrift shop blazers and ties, dragging a duct-taped guitar, an unstrung bass and kicking along a cracked Peavey amp that smells overpoweringly like Southern Comfort. The kid with the flashlight filling a tomato-stained Tupperware bowl with Ruffles immediately starts in going, "Um, okay, see this? This is for Damager. So you guys can't have these, Damager only, got it? You have to get your own—Hey! Hey! Wud I jus' say?! Damager ONLY!"

Oh right, sorry. So where's Damager? Well, over there, that's gotta be the bass player (you can usually or always tell). He's not looking too busy at the moment and he's the only one in the room who looks like he could go either way on the chip business, so he is approached.

"Hey, man. Nice to meet you. We're the band playing before you."

"Yo. I'm Thor. What's up?"

"Not a lot, we're just having some problem like we don't have a drum kit."

Eastern quiet.

"You think we can use yours?"

It must be kept in mind that Damager's drum set was obviously more expensive and complicated than the space shuttle, and we are tiny and drunk. Damager can't comprehend how we could presume to be able to tame their kit, and says no. No drum kit for you. And by the way, you get ten minutes.

(Metal is *don't touch my gear, no chips, ten minutes.* Always.)

First band comes on suddenly with a fucking "pissa" laser show and like fourteen synthesizers and does, you know, that. Then we come out and play a song about drinking on the little guitar kit and some crap we found in the sacristy, dwarfed in front of Damager's towering custom Crates. Then, fuck 'em, we do an extra fifteen minutes of how we think "Fade to Black" goes for pissed-off Thor, the drummer's girlfriend, and Filthy Matilda, the local bag lady. The vibe was getting really bad (no thanks to us, of course). It was occurring to all three of us that Damager might actually kill us. In the end, I think the only reason they didn't kill us was because their spirits must have been broken, broken like a spirit can only break in a church basement. No, it's not easy for Damager. Or us, but look at us: we're the lucky ones—somehow.

I guess something was wrong with the puppet, because we had seen them roll it out the door while we were playing, but we stuck around to check out the puppetless show anyway. They did "Seek and Destroy" and something else. I don't know, but I bet it was also by Metallica. It was all right, but as God as my witness, we were louder. We left before the bag lady, but after the drummer's girlfriend. And so it was at our third gig ever that we decided playing with metal bands sort of sucks.

Eleven years later, I sit backstage at—where are we? Anyway, without exaggeration, I can report that Anthrax *does not have as much equipment as Damager had.*

These shows with this metal band are not so bad, though. We usually play to at least thirty people (there'd probably be more if we could go on after it's dark outside, but what do we need, *more* contempt?) and now we get a full set (well, almost) and some chips, because we're signed. Every night the Fu come out with huge dark riffs and their equipment in working order and people digging it. We come out with regular drinking songs with like three notes in them and a cracked Marshall that smells overpoweringly like Ketel One, people not digging it. Six "yeah, babys" in, some guy goes "you suck" and throws a hot dog or something. And then I light my bass on fire and throw him the goats and then some other guy goes, "I'm gonna fucking kill you," which you can actually hear, because no one's doing anything. Then we go in the room and sit and have the wet pita wedge and the giant cup of liquor we signed our lives away for. Manhattan, Boise, Atlanta, Atlantis, the Moon. Everywhere, it'll be the same. But as always, it could be worse. We could be working at Copy Cat getting chewed out by the new junior manager from Damager. So off we go.

Metal up your ass, or more accurately, up ours.

Cincinnati, Ohio
1/25/00

The dueling banjo cusp of West Virginia is an uncommonly beautiful part of the country. I remember the venue. There's a railed-off center area and it can make things easy a number of ways. The club people are all right. I'm inclined to believe that we were here with Motörhead just last week, but it can't have been. Steve says it's been months.

Cleveland, Ohio
1/26/00

Took casual notice of the itinerary—the venue holds 850, the promoter's HQ is a place called Chagrin Falls. Uh-huh. Sitting in a Hooters in The Flats calculating that we are closing in on our albeit pretty unchallenging goal of eating at all of them. What. It's Steve's goal really, but it appeals because it's possible—unlike say touring successfully for profit. I do wish for less orange and less sports (always), and the waitresses' stockings have a sheen borrowed from a leathery Floridian widow, but that aside, the Caesar salad is consistently not terrible and sometimes you can have edible king crab legs. You can also come to know a great deal about a town by having a conversation with a Hooters girl. She's an augur with salads, and furthermore she has nothing in common with a scowling heavy metal person. Welcome back.

Hooters is a good barometer if you think about it. When a community at large is invited to ogle underpaid women while they eat, who shows up and what they do when they get there says something about what the locals get away with in general. At Hooters in deep Alabama, Kentucky, etc., you see Good Ol' Boys engage in extremely greasy, aggressive waitress leering—unsettling to watch at all, let alone when it's fundamental to moving onion rings. No women or children are ever in these ones. In contrast, Lubbock has the booster seats and crayons at every other table. Then there's the sportscasters' convention spilling shit in Chicago, wisely being eyed by waitresses' boyfriends, loaded like tigers at the back table, ready to pop the first fucker who grabs a handful of orange nylon, and it won't be long.

Pyro is essential. We don't have the budget for it, but that doesn't mean there isn't going to be some shit going off when we play. I have some cheap conical things good for spitting flame and sparks twenty feet up, for outdoor use only, so those don't come out unless we're in a really sizeable joint. The standard one I use nearly always because it's only a little unpredictable, is called the "disco flash"—a tiny clay button with a wick; I tape it to the headstock to be lit at whatever moment feels most dramatic. The moment in Cleveland was the end of a breakdown mid-set. I lit the thing up and it did its thing while we poured ourselves back into the riff. A few seconds later, I saw an itty little fire on the drum rug and stomped it out with only minor difficulty.

Then a bustle was on stage behind me and I turned to see a raging pyre of about two feet in height coming out of the monitor. I go to stomp it out, microphone stand goes over into the front line and pops a kid in the head. I'm stomping fiercely now with a small flame blooming on my pants at the thigh. Still playing, hoping nobody really notices the fire or that it's growing in intensity. Matt looks over suddenly alarmed because something smells like shit.

(One time in Milwaukee, this happened inside the bass drum and I immediately doused it with a beer, destroying a microphone at considerable expense. So not really knowing what kind of damage has occurred already to the monitor, I'm not dumping anything.) Finally, a genius comes up with a wet towel and smothers the monitor out. We keep playing, as giants with laminates are massing in the wings punching their hands, waiting for me to get off stage so the pummeling can ensue. The monitor is charred, and I'm concocting an exit strategy enviable by Spiderman.

Off stage right, Sgt. Slaughter is checking his watch and glaring at me, stage left is the monitor engineer pointing and screaming. Everyone's gonna have to calm down before this can be dealt with properly, so I'm gonna get the fuck out and give 'em time. Steve comes out in a helicopter crouch and screams something into my ear—sounds like "Straight back!" Okay. Big overblown ending on E, dump the bass, disappear behind the drums as three to six booming red behemoths rush the stage. There's a cement wall across the street with a drop of about five or six feet to the riverbank—out the backstage door, bolt for the wall as casually as possible (which is not all that casually) vaulting over onto the grass. It's better if I wait here until such time as I am provided with a situation report.

Debriefed in the van, I'm made aware that everything is cool, kind of, but we're in the hole for the monitor, and maybe it's best if . . . that's fine. I'll just sit here and read take-out menus for a couple hours. When the crowd outside the club is through hovering around the buses and the sidedoor whacks open for load-out, I go over and apologize to the monitor guy. He said no big deal, but you should get back in the van or somewhere not here, now-ish.

What happened, I see now, is that I taped the disco flash too close to where it ignites, the heat melted the duct tape, and so it fell off, expensively, into the monitor. Tape *along the outside* from now on.

Boulder, Colo.
2/1/00

Drive was *hell*. Broke down. It's the tip of the engine failure iceberg, probably. No showers for almost a week now, no horizontal sleep for two and a half days. I am deficient in all categories of health. We all are. My organs hurt. I smell like an animal that's been dead under the porch for a month. We're sitting outside a health food supermarket, about to go in there and pounce on some "One World" remedies.

Have procured two rooms in the area of the college. More like little apartments, really. Inexpensive and very comfortable. For fifteen hours we have unobstructed access to a place with a television, a shower, and a bed. Earlier, in the hippie store, I was eating handfuls of burdock root right out of the plastic bin, imagining feeling rejuvenated with every wooden bite. I subsequently consumed nearly a whole bottle of "high potency" chewable vitamin C, a honey stick with ginseng, some yinchiaos, a twig, chai, two daily multivitamin packets, an assload of milk thistle, and some tofu made by a gypsy, and sat heaving on the bench outside waiting for health to come.

The theater we're playing has sushi at it. We were entitled to ten dollars' worth. We're a mile up, and fed, finally awake. The altitude is of great benefit—dizziness and disorientation in every breath, just the way we like it.

Our dressing room had a shuttered window box suitable for Shakespearean monologues. It's also a good spot to watch six hundred Anthrax fans lose their shit. Fu had a good piece of the room here too, on account of the Colorado "Thunderbud." This worked much to our advantage. We may even have sold a T-shirt. I sat above the fray in a comfortable old armchair in the band loft tapping the bottom of the soy sauce dish over my mouth.

God bless these fucking hippies.

There's a thriving coke scene here. A still life on a cedar table, a special *Mayan* coke plate. Neat lines sized to *avoid* a cardiac event. (Avoid?) A teaspoon *from Djibouti* for the scooping of the snowy little gram from the stone soy sauce dish (Bread & Circus, $6.99). Fabric squares for shining up the spoon. Allowances made for the worry-doll market. The sophisticated mark of Cloud City chic, the casual extravagance of the altitude.

Consider the other towns on the Earth-mother circuit.

Burlington: soy sauce dish from Star Market, teaspoon from heirloom chest. Steer conversation towards lake monster.

Brattleboro: gram not so good, spoon not so much.

Northampton: ditto, plus scratched CD cover and no one has bills to roll up.

Bearsville: don't care where spoon is from, mixing board from England.

Taos: implements turquoise, nice pillows.

Santa Cruz: near pestilence, blow infested with gnats; sprayed with snot by exorcist dealer having paranoid meltdown due to "blow gnats."

See, it really is "One World."

San Diego,
Orange County, Calif.
2/2/00

> ### *"We begin bombing in five minutes . . ."*
> **—President Ronald Reagan**

We have some good friends in San Diego. There's a crew of chaps we usually hang around with at this bar called Joe's. Joe's is one of the all-time great places to get fucked up. As in blindly swinging at parking attendants who aren't parking attendants they're cops fucked up. As in thinking you're in Massachusetts, but can't find Storrow Drive because the palm trees keep jumping into the middle of the road fucked up. As in trying to speak Spanish to women who are not women they're mailboxes fucked up. You play there in a window box. The size and angles of the space would suggest a tight squeeze for a battery-powered waving Santa, but still you squeeze in there and you give them rock.

This time, though, we weren't playing Joe's.

This tour just went from being another day with free bad coffee to being a punishing trek not matched since Hannibal headed for the mountains with elephants and no shoes. Steve's making some calls, but it doesn't look good. There's an overturned golf cart, police cars, Eugene's got a shiner. *Five* minutes to play now? BEFORE THE DOORS OPEN? We drove for two days, spent hundreds of dollars, no food, no showers . . . Well, here we are.

I am going into that bar right there, right now, to get mythically wasted. Watch this.

Goats in the Rearview

Put up last night by a guy called Kenny, who only listened to Queensrÿche—*only*. He lived in an apartment with a bowl, a spoon, and his Queensrÿche albums. Kenny also *only* talked about Queensrÿche, and he wanted to do this tonight. We were fucking exhausted and we don't know from Queensrÿche. He was on something, I pray, when he attempted to engage us with the exacting pantomime routine he had worked out to *Operation: Mindcrime*, which was shaking the windows at four in the morning. Just then his landlords, who he would not confess were his parents, evicted him forcibly. As we pulled away from the curb, Kenny was in the rearview surrounded by all of his shit. He was bewildered. Life would be merciless to Kenny from here on. But he had his hand in the air, throwing the goats. Metal.

8

Letters and Science

Dead Letter Office

2/03/00
FUCKING MEMO

RE: NO MORE BULLSHIT
TO WHOM IT OBVIOUSLY DOES NOT CONCERN
(EVERYONE)

SUBJECT: MENDING WAYS

FROM: THE UNBAND

CC: YOUR MOTHER YOU FUCKING KNUCKLEHEAD
FUCKING FUCKS

ATTENTION:

   CONTAINED IN THE FOLLOWING PAGES ARE
THINGS OF CONCERN ONLY TO PERSONS WHO
ARE IN A POSITION TO DO SOMETHING ABOUT
THEM—BUT ONE MIGHT BE ENCOURAGED TO
EXAMINE ONE'S POSITION BECAUSE THIS SHIT IS
GETTING SERIOUSLY *FUCKED* UP—AND NOT IN
THE GOOD WAY.

TRAVEL:

Distances, routes, and costs will be determined in a precise manner with careful considerations given regarding *EXPENSES*. Ask YOURSELF AND INVOLVED PARTIES:

- DOES THE SHOW/TOUR pay? IF SO HOW MUCH DOES IT PAY? (SIMPLE, NO?)

- ARE WE GOING TO BE FED AND GIVEN AT LEAST ONE DRINK AT SOME POINT BEFORE, DURING, OR AFTER THE SHOW/TOUR?

- IS THE AMOUNT OF $ IT WILL COST US TO PLAY THE SHOW/TOUR MORE THAN THE AMOUNT OF MONEY WE MAKE BY PLAYING THE WEEK OF SHOWS TO FOLLOW?

- WHAT IS IT, AGAIN, THAT I ACTUALLY DO FOR THIS BAND?

FROM NOW ON: THE ANSWERS TO THE PREVIOUS QUESTIONS WILL BE DETERMINED BY USE OF A) NON-FICTIONAL INFORMATION AND B) A FUCKING *MACHINE WHICH IS MEANT FOR THE JOB* (NOT A FUCKING *NINTENDO*). ACCEPTABLE MACHINES INCLUDE <u>CALCULATORS, ADDING MACHINES, CHINAMAN WITH FUCKING ABACUS, AND ESPECIALLY COMPUTERS</u> WHICH ARE AVAILABLE TO THE PUBLIC THESE DAYS. I SAW A DUCK WITH A LAPTOP THE OTHER DAY, AND *HIS* SHIT LOOKED PRETTY FUCKING SORTED.

NATURALLY WE CANNOT HOPE TO ALWAYS BE MAKING $ BUT AT LEAST: IS OUR RELATIONSHIP WITH THE BAND WITH WHOM WE SHARE THE BILL

GOING TO BE A WELCOME ONE? (WE DO NOT NEED TO PAY TO MAKE FRIENDS.)

IS THE VENUE A REAL PLACE? IS IT STILL OPEN? (YOU KNOW WHAT THE FUCK I'M TALKING ABOUT.)

THE NECESSARY PORTION OF THE TOUR BUDGET WILL BE RELEASED TO THE TRAVELING PARTY SO THAT I CAN STOP FUCKING HAVING TO CALL MY *MOTHER* TO BORROW MONEY AT THE BEGINNING OF EVERY FUCKING TOUR. WHATEVER ANYBODY THINKS ABOUT THE "DRUG PROBLEM," YOU'RE *FUCKING* WRONG. WE NEED *BASIC TOOLS OF THE TRADE AND A WORKING VEHICLE.* IT'S THE FUCKING UP OF THESE *FUCKING* NECESSITIES THAT FUCKS THE TOUR.

BUDGET WILL BE RELEASED TO THE BAND IN FAIR TIME TO:

- PURCHASE FUELS TO RUN THE TOURING VEHICLES

- HAVE THE VEHICLE(S) INSPECTED SO AS TO BE LEGAL

- RENT THINGS WE NEED (I HAD TO LEAVE MY *FUCKING CAR* WITH THE U-HAUL GUY AS COLLATERAL. IF SOMETHING GOES SOUR, WHO WILL GET THE SHORT END OF THE STICK DO YOU THINK?)

- PAY OFF PARKING TICKETS RECEIVED WHILE THE BAND IS LOADING/UNLOADING EQUIP-MENT OR *PERFORMING* SO THAT THE VAN DOES NOT GET BOOTED

- DANGEROUS MECHANICAL PROBLEMS WILL BE TENDED TO *PRIOR* TO TRAVEL.

THE UNBAND IS VERY FUCKING LUCKY TO HAVE LIVED AS LONG AS THEY HAVE. WE SHOULDN'T PUSH IT UNLESS IT IS AN EXCEPTIONAL IDEA TO DO SO AND DRIVING THROUGH NARROW MOUNTAIN PASSES AT PSYCHOTIC GRADES IN ICE STORMS WITH NO WIPERS AND IFFY BRAKES AND ONE FUCKING HEADLIGHT SO WE CAN PLAY A TACO RESTAURANT IS NOT AN EXCEPTIONAL IDEA, AND ANY OF US CAN ASSURE THE HOME OFFICE THAT IF WE HAD ENOUGH FOOD IN OUR STOMACHS TO SHIT WITH FEAR, THEY WOULD FIND IT ON THEIR DOORSTEPS.

NO MONEY BEFORE TOUR = BAD. DANGEROUS VAN, DEATH LOOMS.

MONEY BEFORE TOUR = GOOD, SAFE VAN, DEATH LOOMS BUT ONLY IN THE USUAL, SENSIBLE WAY.

VAN:

UNLESS UNDER ATTACK BY FLYING MONKEYS THE VAN IS TO BE CLEANED EVERY FOUR DAYS AS TO RENDER IT *CLEANER THAN IT WAS BEFORE.* GENERALLY THE VAN SHOULD BE:

- NO LONGER SMELLING LIKE SOME FUCKING THING FROM A FUCKING ASS

- VACCUUMED

SHOW ADVANCEMENTS/ BOOKING
MORE QUESTIONS:

- DOES THE VENUE KNOW WE'RE COMING?

- DO THEY *WANT* US TO COME?

- DO THEY KNOW WHAT KIND OF BAND WE ARE?

(HINT: **NOT A REGGAE BAND**)

IF SO, THEN:

- HAS THE TECHNICAL RIDER BEEN SENT? HOW ABOUT THE HOSPITALITY RIDER? HAVE THE PEOPLE WHO NEED TO SEE THOSE SEEN THEM?

- DO THEY KNOW THAT WE WILL BE POSSIBLY LIGHTING FIRES? IS A GIANT GOING TO COME AND TAKE SOMEBODY'S HEAD OFF BECAUSE HE "NEVER WOULD HAVE ALLOWED THAT IF HE HAD BEEN *TOLD*?"

- IS THE NAME OF OUR BAND GOING TO BE DIS-PLAYED IN ANY WAY THAT WILL RELATE TO THE CROWD THAT THIS PERFORMANCE IS BY A GROUP CALLED THE UNBAND?

GUEST LISTS:

WHEN THE BAND AND TOUR MANAGER NEED TO BE PRESENT AT A SHOW, THESE PERSONS SHOULD:

A) BE ALLOWED TO GET IN WITHOUT HASSLE

B) THERE IS NO FUCKING B

INTERVIEWS/PRESS CALLS:

THE BAND SHOULD BE MADE AWARE THAT SUCH THINGS ARE HAPPENING WITH ONE (1) HOUR'S NOTICE IF POSSIBLE, BUT NO LESS THAN FIFTEEN MINUTES. WHY?

THERE ARE TWO PROBLEMS THAT FREQUENTLY OCCUR WITH THE UNBAND, AS I'M SURE WE ALL KNOW TOO WELL. ONE IS THAT THEY ARE *SMASHED.* TWO IS THAT THEY ARE *NOT SMASHED.* BOTH OF THESE PROBLEMS CAN BE MINIMIZED BY OBSERVING THAT

A) A PERSON CAN DEFINITELY BE OKAY IN AN HOUR, EVEN FOR COURT

B) A PERSON CAN GET *FUCKED UP* IN FIFTEEN MINUTES, BUT NOT USUALLY IN TEN

MONEY:

HA HA HA HA HA HA HA! YEAH FUCKING RIGHT!

AT THE *LEAST* ALL BAND MEMBERS ARE TO HAVE FIVE (5) DOLLARS IN THEIR POCKETS AT ALL TIMES. PERIOD. THAT IS ABOUT AS MUCH AS MOST HOMELESS PERSONS HAVE AS A RESULT OF *BEGGING CHANGE ON THE STREET.* WE DO NOT EXPECT GIANT SUMS FROM OUR "RECORDING CONTRACT" WITH THE "MAJOR INDIE" BUT IF EVERYONE IN THE ORGANIZATION COULD TAKE A FUCKING SECOND TO UNDERSTAND WHAT HAPPENS WHEN A BAND MEMBER GETS SEPARATED AND SUFFERS MALNUTRITION IN A STRANGE CITY AND HAS TO BUM CHANGE *OFF OF A FUCKING CRACK ADDICT* (THIS IS *NOT* HYPOTHETICAL) AND THEN CALLING NEW YORK OR LOS ANGELES, SINCE THERE APPEARS TO BE *NO GOD* AFTER ALL, TO BE TOLD SOMETHING ABOUT *"UNITS"* OR *"ADDS"* BUT NOT FUCKING SANDWICHES. *PLEASE* MAY WE HAVE *FIVE FUCKING DOLLARS* OF OUR "OWN" MONEY?

ALL RECEIPTS AND EXPENDITURES WILL BE RE-CORDED AND CALCULATED IN A WAY WHICH IS:

A) VISIBLE

   AND

B) TANGIBLE

EQUIPMENT:

THE EQUIPMENT BUDGET WAS SPENT THUSLY:

A GUITAR
A MARSHALL HALF STACK
A MARSHALL COMBO
INSTRUMENT REPAIR AND SET-UPS
CYMBALS AND HARDWARE
A TUNER. NOTICE THAT WORD IS NOT PLURAL.
THAT'S ALL.
TOUR EQUIPMENT BUDGET: $0
HMM. WHAT'S MISSING?
BASS AMPS OR DRUMS WOULD BE NICE BUT FAILING THAT STRINGS, PICKS, AND STICKS.

THANK YOU.

BY THE WAY, WE ARE GOING TO HAVE A "MEET-ING" AND ANYONE WHO HAS NOT BEEN TRAVEL-ING WITH US FOR MORE THAN THREE WEEKS IS TO KEEP THEIR FUCKING MOUTH SHUT UNTIL WE'RE FINISHED TALKING.

XO,

THE MOTHERFUCKIN UNBAND

Why Do You Think They Call It Hope?

HEY GUYS!

WHAT'S UP? MY NAME'S CHELSEA AND I TURNED FIFTEEN LAST WEEK! I LIVE IN A SMALL TOWN CALLED PACIFIC GROVE AND IT SUCKS! I HEARD ABOUT YOUR SHOW LAST WEEK AT THE SHORE-LINE AND I WANTED TO GO, BUT IT WAS ALL SOLD OUT. EVERYONE LOVES YOUR BAND AROUND HERE, BUT ME MOST OF ALL! OH MY GOD YOU ARE SOOOOOOOOOO HOT! YOUR BAND HAS THE COOLEST NAME. DO YOU HAVE ANY WIVES? DID YOU ALWAYS KNOW YOU WOULD BE MUSICIANS? IF NOT, WHAT DID YOU THINK YOU WOULD BE? WHAT DO YOU DO FOR EXCITEMENT? I LIKE TO DO WHATEVER IS FUN! HAVE YOU EVER DONE SOME-THING THAT MADE YOU TOTALLY EMBARRASSED? HAVE YOU EVER BEEN TOTALLY SCARED? WHAT IS YOUR FAVORITE COLOR? WHAT IS YOUR FAVORITE FOOD?

MOST IMPORTANT QUESTION: WHAT'S THE MEANING OF LIFE?

I CAN'T FIGURE IT OUT.

XOXO,
CHELSEA

Dearest Chelsea,

I'm so glad you wrote! We love hearing from fans! We'd be nothing without fans, and therefore: *I'd* be nothing without *you*! You know, I've been to Pacific Grove and you're right! It *does* suck! I'm sorry you didn't get to go to the concert, but thank you for writing so promptly! We'll be back to the Shoreline, and by that time we might be a little less popular, and you'll be able to get a ticket no problem. As a matter of fact I'll let you in on a secret, Chelsea—I'm working on an album right now that's going to make us *very* unpopular indeed. So don't worry!

Well no, Chelsea, I didn't always want to be in a band—especially not a wildly successful *money machine* like this one! What a pain in the butt! No, my Dream was to wander the earth eating canned food from ninety-nine cent stores, dreaming. But you know what, Chelsea? If you keep reaching and reaching and reaching and reaching, and reaching, and reaching, and reaching, and reaching, and reaching, and reaching, and reaching, and reaching, and *reaching* just a little more, someday not too long after that, something that doesn't require reaching hardly at all will come along and give you the conditional opportunity to reach a little more! Now that's what I call hope!

My favorite things to do are:

1. Not die!

I feel sooo stupid because I can't think of anything else! But coincidentally I like fun things too! That's pretty weird, huh? The most embarrassing thing I've ever done? Well, I'm sorry to say it's my last record! I don't know *what* I was thinking! You know like if your yearbook picture *really really* sucks? Well it's like that, but way way worse, cuz it's like, the *world* yearbook. You know what I mean?

The scariest thing that's ever happened? That's easy! You might be too young to remember this, but one time the President of The United States was Ronald Reagan, and he came on the radio and said that our country was about to launch nuclear missiles at Russia. That would kill millions of people and make the earth uninhabitable for generations! But really it was a joke! We weren't doing that at all, it's just that The President of The United States thought wouldn't it be *funny* if we *were*! Well, that takes the cake for me, Chelsea. That is the scariest thing that ever happened—unless you've been to Space Mountain! Have you? I haven't! My favorite color is blue, and my favorite food is any!

As for your last question, I can't say that I totally know the answer, even though my *huge* recording contract does allow a philosophical latitude not available to most mortals—and I mean that in the *best* possible way! We *love* mortals! We'd be nothing without them! Anyway, I do know this—and promise me you'll read the *whole* sentence, not just the first part, okay?

Life has no meaning, and that's *good*.

If it did, Chelsea, not only would we have to *act along*, but worse, it would be used to market soap.

Anyway, gotta go! The Brinks truck is here! (I *hate* carrying my wallet!) See you next time we're at the Shoreline!

XO,
M. Ruffino

9

Nobody Else Is Dio

```
┌─────────────────────────────────┐
│                                 │
│        DIO & THE UNBAND         │
│          U.S. TOUR              │
│       MARCH–APRIL, 2000         │
│                                 │
└─────────────────────────────────┘
```

*It is a land of many villages and towns, amply
stocked with the means of life. It affords good
sport with all sorts of wild game. . . . The climate,
however, is unhealthy: it is, in fact, extremely
enervating. Hence, the nobility of the country, who
used to be men of valour and stalwart soldiers, are
now craven, and excel at nothing but drinking.*

—*Marco Polo*, The Travels

Making Room

Northampton, Mass.
3/20

We left a day late, but it had nothing to do with the fact
that we tried to leave from a bar. We were having electrical

problems, and so was the van—no directionals, no head-lights, and *vapors*. Plus nobody is a licensed driver, plus drinking. Next time maybe we won't stop at the bar. Unfor-tunately, losing a day means we will be fucking ourselves with less than enough hours to get to Seattle. So we would certainly leave at, or about at, the crack of dawn.

The blowback from the Texas Incident is a bit more ghoulish than one might have expected, as a *videotape* has surfaced and this is not "good for business," they tell us. The label has "one foot out the door," taken to mean that things are a little Probationary right now. We have come a hair's breadth of destroying our career before we even get a chance to destroy it properly. We might surmise that there isn't any room for fuck-ups.

Not Morning People

3/21

Managed to get underway around noon, for very good rea-sons that escape me at the moment. I do remember that we had some shit said to us and then there was some *spackling*. Matt can only communicate in insulting hand gestures. I took four pills and three Irish coffees, so I'm okay so long as no one looks at me or talks to me or comes near me. Eugene is sleeping in the back.

Very special brand of punctuality displeased Steve once again, which we were prepared for—mostly. Steam was coming out of his ears when we pulled up. He chucked a box of our T-shirts off the second floor balcony, which exploded on the windshield of the van and littered the street with merch. Matt wandered off to get a taco.

It was discovered that we have locked our equipment in the trailer with an old lock for which we did not have a key. We secured a pair of bolt cutters from the local black-smith, but the lock proved to be a challenge. The violence of the project sated Steve a little, but the bolt cutters were destroyed. This resulted in the first Getaway of the Tour. You hear the yelling, you get in the van, no questions.

Right now we're on the side of the highway completely out of gas. "Girl from Ipanema" is on the radio, which is bungeed to the console.

U-Hole

Electrical difficulties were partially resolved at a monstrous U-Haul joint in Albany, but still no proper radio. Eugene and I had a secret beer at a Pizza Hut in a Dakota. The joke about no drinks until Seattle is not so funny on account that Steve was not joking, and he's got all the fucking money. We would very much like to get to Seattle.

Made extremely good time through Montana, where there is no speed limit beyond what is reasonably safe for a van full of unlicensed drivers in various stages of alcohol withdrawal dragging an overloaded and unregistered trailer on bald tires.

Sicilian Sketch

3/23

Woke up on the floor of the van, where I have learned to arrange myself for sleep in a way that improves on the usual method of sleeping sitting up pretzeled in the captain's chair. The sun's coming up in a mountain pass somewhere in Idaho.

I know a story that goes something like this:

There once was a man from Ragusa (with whom I share a name). He left his lucrative job as a shepherd in the hills of Sicily and pegged it for Jersey. He left his wife after the war, disappearing into a mist of broken English, marauding Italianly, and starting families in trailer parks. He resurfaced only once and appeared to his abandoned wife, sons, and daughter, already a ghost. Then he went off and became, quite impossibly, the sheriff of some half-deserted county in Arizona, spurs, buckles and boots. Sicilian off the boat. Two years pass, and then he's found bludgeoned to death in the front seat of an accordioned Lincoln—it had been rolled from a giant cliff.

It would bode well for this range to have been his last sight. Because this is fucking *nice*.

Watertown Shadow

Seattle, Wash.
3/23

Fifty-three hours, fifty-nine minutes from the AAA Road Service guy in Mass. to the door of the club. It is an old firehouse, and the building itself, spiritually, has a mullet: a "Kentucky Waterfall" as some say. Our own name for the hairstyle came from years back and seems to be peculiar to the Boston area. The closest Registry of Motor Vehicles for us was in a place called Watertown, so that's where we all went to get our licenses so we could legally drive ah fatha's cahs down ta Wompatuck fa tha kegga. The plus was that in Watertown you didn't have to wait as long as at the downtown Boston office, the minus was that when you got your picture taken, a strange shadow would appear on either side of your neck that would look like a mullet. Nothing you could do. Business in the front, party in the back until your license expires. This was "The Watertown Shadow." These are not shadows here though. This crowd, in a line around the block, is up and down with world-class ape drapes.

I don't think there's a P.A. here yet, preventing soundchecks. That seems like something that would *not* happen to Dio, but speaking from experience, the sheer number of mullets here would indicate that something unprofessional is afoot. We are going for a Bloody Mary at the place that puts sardines in them.

Met a label rep who freely admits to not liking our music excepting "Cocaine Whore" and the Squire cover because the rest of the record is "stupid beer drinking party rock." We all just stared at the guy. *Exactly.*

An older crowd here, naturally, who maybe don't get out that often, but when they do: Fuck. And fucking a, b, and c if it's Ronnie James Dio. That's an Audience. They like to get *possessed.* And there are *women* at the Dio show. Several even. Of course, it doesn't seem like a miracle that there'd be a lady at a metal show unless you'd been touring with a useless, plodding sausage party like say, oh I don't know . . . *Anthrax.* No one chucked anything particularly dangerous at us, we loaded up, had a few beers and returned victoriously to the hotel with our vegetable platter.

Someone had scrawled "DEO ROCKS" on the back of our trailer.

Jimi Hat

Aurora Ave. is a vine of filthy motels and windowless porn shops. However, the Marco Polo Motel is very clean because its proprietors fear God. And, it would seem, us. A pleasant enough couple, one very thin and one very not so. Not really sure what they're about beyond tapping the tourist pamphlets back into order. They have this small and oddly shaved dog-type animal with its jaw wired shut who runs around making noises like a thing in the woods at night.

This is of course excellent.

The "cable television" advertised on the marquee,

typically enough, meant "barely UPN," so we wound up watching some movie about basketball. Golf is less useless, on account of the little drinking car.

Watched Maury Povich, his guests had Tourette's. Unlike most people, they say the right thing a couple times a day.

Took a shower, got lost on buses for some hours trying to find a Tower Records. Found everyone back at the club. They'd all been to Jimi Hendrix's grave. Eugene left him a drink ticket from the Continental and Matt left him an extra large condom.

Place is filled with five hundred persons. Some unexpected—actually that's bullshit, we always expect it—arrangement came through resulting in too much drugs. Forgot about what I'd already taken, which I did for the purpose of concealing it from the authorities. Not *too* sure about the pharmacology there, but as we say, "Eh. Should be fine."

Creeping Jesus at the Underlook Motel

By some total miracle, or more likely something Steve did, we got loaded out and made it to a Motel 6. We opened another bottle of Ketel and I went for ice.

I'm perpetually going for ice in dicey motels, but this one is not like the others: one would expect any moment to be passed by a headless maid pushing a squeaky cart full of medical equipment and shrunken monkey heads.

I was full of chemical valor and the cause of More Drink, and so was off wobbling towards the vending machines. The window screen at the end of the hall had been removed and propped against the wall; a hotel phone dangled over the sill, having just been used to strangle a prostitute. The carpet's jumping a bit. There's a trail of bloody Q-tips, leading to four Girl Scouts smoking crack. There is no fucking ice machine and I'm never going home.

This motel looked so small from the highway, but I have been wandering for *hours*. The fluorescent lights aren't helping and the fucking bees and snakes aren't either. Whore laughter is coming from somewhere. Then, as a ten-foot swell of carpet comes toward me, everything just *goes*. The walls melt, the hammer comes down, and—yup, here we go. That's the stuff all right, just what I was afraid of: evil hippie shit in the biker drugs. I contemplated lying down right there because: (a) this is what I did in department stores as a hapless toddler; (b) those Girl Scouts have crack and they might walk by; and (c) gentlemanly repose.

Whatever remained of the man I once was persevered and found the vending area. There was the grail, humming gloriously, ready to give ice. Perfect, except that the door's locked.

Pulled together as best I could, went around to the registration office to see what could be done. The Night Clerk, who had a crow on his shoulder, did not know shit for English, so far as I could tell (my own grip of the language was loose at the time too). I asked as best I could for a key for the drinking and eating stuff machine place. "I must get to the far bins," or something. He understood the key part at least and asked me which room I was in. Having no fucking clue, I say very confidently "two-fifty-nine," thinking he just needs to know that I'm a guest of the hotel. He steps just out of view and comes back and hands me a key card. "Ice, right?" he shakes his head and takes the card back. He writes "259" on it with a marker. Wait. He made *me* a fucking key to somebody's *room*.

I must look a little more respectable than the usual drugged-out psychotic on an ice hunt. I stared at the key. Thought about saying, "Thanks. And while you're at it I could use the keys to 146, 234, 134, and do you have anything to get bloodstains out?" but I just said, "No, the *far bin machine room*. Back over up in there. With the ice." When I did eventually reach the ice machine, the mission to scoop the ice into the bucket involved fantastic inefficiencies.

The trek back to the room was improbably successful. I went in and sat down at the table with the ice bucket on my lap. A quietly drunken card game was in progress. Matt put down his hand, walked over and casually took a handful of ice, tossed it in a plastic cup, and dumped four fingers of Ketel and a splash of cranberry over it. He had a sip which he followed with a satisfied sigh, unknowingly slamming shut the book of shadows, Motel 666 edition, in a cloud of mummy-dust.

Shanghai'd

Portland, Ore.

Portland this morning is all about Mai Tai. Mai Tai, Mai Tai, Mai Tai, Mai Tai. We try going to Hung Far Lo but it's closed. Over to another Chinese joint which is inexplicably called Vinnie's and has a plastic Italian pizza guy statue out front. The hostess, lying, tells us a bartender will be happy to serve us at the back bar. A couple of families are at tables. We sit at the bar in total silence for a few minutes (Need Mai Tai.) This goes on for around five more minutes, no one coming. Steve squeezes out a fart—an unhappy little frog launching off the vinyl stool and ricocheting around the room. He jumps on the bar and screams, "IS THERE A BARTENDER IN THE HOOS!?!?!?", jumps down and shoots out the door. Somebody drops a chopstick. Our work is done here.

We're on I-5 in northern California. Need Alka-Seltzer. Spent an extra night in Portland drinking all over the place.

Could've stayed there another week and been quite happy I think, *relaxing* at The Space Room. The Space Room is usually headquarters because they have Bloody Marys yet to be matched in the contiguous forty-eight, and we have known ourselves to drink in there for twelve hours straight. This time, maybe four hours in, there was a shift change. The new waitress checked our IDs (we were fucking hammered at a table full of empty glasses, but hey, go ahead). She noted with some surprise where we were from. Then there were phone calls made and within minutes, all of western Massachusetts's whatever-happened-to's arrived. Thus began the actual drinking, for Old Time's sake—the recidivist's mantra.

The whole posse tumbled around the corner after last call, to Eugene's old girlfriend's boyfriend's cousin's brother's friend's apartment, where everyone was initially asleep. Lots of gin (to which none of us are normally inclined) and acoustic guitars (likewise), but what can you do. Had a few glasses of wine after the gin ran out then went out for cocktails at the something or other. Back to the apartment of the girl who brought the wine to the other place—the one with the coat with the fur on it—and finished off the surprise Wild Turkey stash. Cooked several omelets and managed to get a Stones album on before passing out hopelessly fucked in the middle of the room. Left around something A.M. I may have gotten to the van by my own power. Possibly (likely) I was again removed from the apartment into the dawn, fireman-style, by Steve.

Gypsies, Tramps and Thieves

San Francisco, Calif.

The club is called Maritime Hall it turns out because the building contains the offices of the seafarer's unions and such. It is in sections portholed. Model ships in cases in the lobby, janitors swabbing long shiny hallways, silence. There's a destroyed hippie outside the place showing off a "Marijuana Permit."

Hospitality guy is done up well. He has dressed himself with obvious care to invoke the spirit of Pill Elvis. He is consistent in the bringing of carrots and beer and says things like "the platypus is go." He's prancing around in a crooked wig.

People go fucking *apeshit* tonight: Dio has chosen to break out "Last in Line." The kind of apeshit that—well, here: at the last show a gentleman with an All Access backstage pass related to me a story of how Ronnie James literally saved his wife's life by personally coming to her hospital room. In almost every town you hear tales of amazing unselfish acts performed by Ronnie (and Wendy) on a personal level. He is known for this. Anyway, this guy insisted *emphatically* that he would lie down in front of a train for Dio, and then asked me to propose other sacrificial acts he could perform for Dio. Jump off a building? Yup. Eat glass? Yup. And so on. He is not alone, by any stretch.

Then—for the first time in forever—Dio busts into the *hit*. Now, people might get pumped up for "Metal Health" at the Quiet Riot reunion, but Kevin DuBrow was not so much with the hospitals, and the list goes on. *Nobody* else is Dio.

In the end, Maritime Hall refuses to pay us. Outright. Just, "no," unapologetically. We hear eventually that this is not unusual, but Steve wisely waited until we were on the road to tell us this. We would have at least done the promoters an inconvenience or two had we known (I'm reminded of touring in an RV a few years ago and opening up its sewage drain onto the entryway of an uncooperative club in Atlanta). Eugene wants to go back for a bit of the ultraviolence, but we're too tired for anything but weak self-assurances that we'll see that money tomorrow. It's the same promoter. Oh yes, we'll get paid.

Santa Crews

Some dirty son of a bitch is walking around downtown Santa Cruz all day screaming at a giant bag of stolen sub rolls: "FUCK YOU FUCK! YOU FUCKIN KNOW IT? YOU DON'T KNOW IT *I* KNOW IT! SHUT UP! SHUT UP! SHUT UP!" Then he takes a bite and spits it out, leaving chunks of bread all over Main Street. Santa Cruz has a lot of these types.

Matt lost his laminate at a sports bar earlier. He pleaded for its return to the very confused Dio crowd. Nobody says shit. Right: if any of you finds a *bag of money*, please give it here.

Dio's gear leaves us about a foot square to set up in. The crew thinks this is very funny. Turns out the club had earlier decided that there would be no opening band, or at the very least if there were one, they would have no P.A. and no money given to them. Wendy Dio tore into the appropriate people appropriately and the Dio crew spent an extra long time setting equipment straight all on our behalf. This is good people.

Previous to this place (which is not so well liked by many a road person we gather), the finest catering had been at the Warfield in San Fran, on account of hippies. This tops it, on account of Asians. It's a copious and sophisticated buffet stocked with foods from distant memory; seaweed salad, cold sesame noodles, sashimi, etc. We ate ourselves sick immediately and then, along with everyone else, hovered around it gluttonously for the better part of an hour.

Sometimes even a light snack within four hours of a show can be a serious mistake, and gorging at any point

after breakfast is flat-out suicide; but *good edible food*—
you jam it the fuck in there when you can. We play, a little
sluggish with fish and all, but the food was not to any otherwise noticeable detriment, a testament to its quality. We
are then, astoundingly, paid. In response to a threat cen-
tered on chopsticks and somebody's sphincter, Steve col-
lects our money from last night. And so it goes. Dio.

House of Booze

L.A., Calif.

There's a lot you can say about the Houses of Blueses.
What I mean is: most, now I am not saying *all*, but *most*
old bluesmen do not, as is my understanding, sit on their
porches in the sweltering Delta stapling bottlecaps to their
furniture. But you're either in Kansas with a flappy pickle
thing with a bug on it drinking a pissed-in Mr. Pibb, or
you're not.

> Steve: "At least I know I'm not gonna have to fight
> for a bottle of vodka from fucken. . . . Worcester."

Another sold-out show and we get nice and messed up
with a bunch of people in the dressing room until the staff
gets nervous. Then there was some reportedly very enter-
taining encounter with Jack Black on the mezzanine, the
addition of a number of druggy people to the van, the pro-
curement of several gallons of vodka, and the usual collapse
onto various floors and couches at dawn.

What Is and What Should Never Be

Picked up a copy of *Hit Parader* today to see what they are
saying about us. It's a kind article making it quite clear that
we are NOT playing at something called "rocket science."

Fine. Neither is NASA. For the sixth anniversary of Kurt Cobain's suicide, they have him featured as the centerfold dressed like it's laundry day as usual, but his photo is cut in half by a pull-out poster of a band who are all wearing masks and proclaiming in pull-quote, "We Are Not Afraid to Be Who We Are!"

Sir, I'm Afraid I'm Going to Have to Ask You to Please Exit the Dragon

The sun is coming up and Los Angeles is a wet sack of broken glass. Or I am. Anyway, a lot of things are wet and many more are broken. I'm sitting in a wrecked kitchen smoking a Winston, though I quit months ago—in Sweden.

L.A.'s funny. Sometimes you black out in the Ripley's Believe It or Not Museum and get tossed out by a guy dressed as Paul Bunyan while protesting that you are The World's Drunkest Man and have just as much right to be there as he does. Then you're at Ralph's in East L.A. employing ancient military strategy to get the beer to the car; then, back to the rehearsal room, so you can drink the beer, not having a window or anything to do. One hour later, you're roasting in your coat on the beach in a tequila coma. If it's good, sometimes you wind up at the Chateau pool majestically eating jumbo shrimp with an actress.

Then, sometimes, you're in a small kitchen, smoking.

Soon it was sunset and time for cocktails with pirates at another shit-hole on Venice Beach. Then time for Twin Dragon, figure we'll get a little messed up on Zombies.

Ten of us there, buzzing a little but no one's throwing spareribs, possibly because they have not yet arrived to the table. The table behind us has a spanking new *Academy Award* standing in the middle of it. Rob snatches this "Oscar" from the table—not without charm. He did sort of an Indiana Jones thing, replacing it with an egg roll. The act in itself is very surprising to the people, rather alarming in fact. The people would be again surprised if they knew that a rain of spareribs was about to assault them for no reason.

I got separated again tonight sometime between The Dragon and the shopping cart incident (I just remember the wheel falling off and that terrible *crunch*, the rest—eh, not so much) and wound up falling all over some tiki joint with total strangers I thought I knew, then Tarzan-ing on cellphones, trying to find the strangers I did know. Heckled a swing band for the duration of a drink. Possibly there was a "disco" portion of the evening where something bad happened. Actually, I'm pretty certain about that. Then everyone was found again, quite by accident, in the process of being ejected by valets. Someone was holding a broken giant palm leaf. Still more strangers with drugs and cellphones and then a topless club. Not the foggiest notion of what the fuck had happened, was happening, or was going to happen. Somebody must've had some grip though, because I'm here and alive. I do remember falling off a stool at the topless club while trying to order, I think, a *mescaline* salad.

It's morning now, but there is vodka left. Let's have one. Everyone's passed out on the living-room floor of Busty Balloon's Westwood digs—it looks like a bunch of hobos snuck into a mass grave.

That's Just My Baby Daddy

Today began with a planet-scorching hangover and a terrible *beeping* somewhere, probably from a truck, which should be made to explode immediately, before my head does. The television is on. It's Maury Povich.

Mr. Povich is addressing everyone like infants. He's undeterred even by the particularly messy life of his guest this morning, a leviathan woman named Shayna. Shayna's in the throes of a great confusion concerning the identity of the father of her child.

The child is a mute pea, and looks basically as content as any baby, while on her behalf a vast collection of gentlemen succumbs to paternity tests. When these men "fail" (as they all do, outing history's greatest slut, God love her), they whoop and punch the air. One guy is pointing, his face two inches from Shayna's, "Not the *father! Not* the father! That's right, *bitch*!"—a quick break to do his best Clubber Lang shadowboxing for the audience—and back to his shouting. Behind the new king of the planet, the big monitor shows a live feed from the orphan cam in the greenroom, wherein Shadiamond wriggles like a mephitic turtle in her frayed nest of dumpster chamois.

One by one, noisily, the suitors depart the soundstage, and Shayna is reunited with her baby and ladled back into the roiling broth of criminally untelevised human misery.

If I may humbly submit my own khaki pants/Dockers/ sweater summary, and I think I will, I think Mr. *Povich* and his voodoo cartel of *c*unts (conversationally speaking) may have "morals" confused with *ethics*.

Adios, Motherfucker
The Slippery Slope and the Inland Empire

There's a special drink made at the Crossroads Bar and Grille in Yucaipa, California which has five kinds of rum in it—they call it the AMF. Adios Mother Fucker. The room here's got an open roof. Sound: good. People: good. A very good band called Unida. Don't quite have a handle on who everyone is in the desert rock scene, but it seems all more or less sired by Kyuss, and step-fathered by Fu when Kyuss broke up. The Unida singer wears a fine cowboy hat.

A girl who won Dio tickets on the radio saw our band, and was brought backstage by the biker security. She was very impressed and wanted to know which one of us was Dio. I think it wound up being Eugene that was Dio.

The shrimp cocktail here is indisputably Sea Monkeys served with ketchup.

Anyway, five kinds of rum.

> *The truth is this. When a man is riding by night through this desert and something happens to make him loiter and lose touch with his companions . . . he hears Spirits talking in such a way that they seem to be his companions. Often these voices make him stray from the path, so that he never finds it again.* —Marco Polo, The Travels

Tour-ettes

As I sit at home comfortably on the porch with tea and greyhounds, I must confess that I completely lost my mind for a period of approximately three and a half days following some mismeasurements in southern California. Matt,

only somewhat less dangerously, was completely fucked with collapsed everything in the back of the van for the same period. Now I am not a stranger to blackouts, whiteouts, deafness, paralysis, etc. and feel singularly equipped to deal with the lot of them with one eye closed and a hand tied back. *But.* What happened in the desert was a breakdown of such horror that I would have at any moment preferred death. I became a spitting incubus, hunched and swearing, chewing on the seat, and talking to phantoms. Point being, I can't vouch for the next few days, nor can I ably describe what happened to me in that very strange place called the Inland Empire.

Lubbock or Leave It
Republic of Texas, U S of A

Matt: "Even prison would be cool if you could just drink all the time."

A Day Off

Lubbock is fucked. Spent the entire day and night at the hotel bar: a day "off." At some point Eugene and I ran into Ronnie James Dio in the elevator and he was saying something about happy hour, so . . . there we go. Ronnie, in response to our need for advice on how to survive the road, sent a guy hiking out to the mall to pick up special Dio vitamins, on him. We were examining them by dusk, taking a few and thanking him. Dio's what, over thirty most likely, but the guy's in Olympian condition, rocking stupendously. Therefore, his advice is taken straight no chaser, though the vitamins are chased with Jaegermeister.

The Miss America tryouts were going on in the adjacent ballroom, and there's an OPEC conference beginning to show itself in our lobby bar. Ronnie and his personal attendant guy named Willy (excellent, British) bought us a couple rounds and the crew started showing up, everyone hunkering down as if into the cockpit of the most powerful drinking plane in the world. There's a locomotive whistle in the distance. In its draft, a rail rat hoists himself into a boxcar carrying a sack containing (a) a number of candelabras and (b) all the restraint in Lubbock.

We wrecked that hotel that night. Badly, provoking repeated, armed room invasions by *personnel* of all shapes, sizes, and demeanors. Matt and Eugene, I think, stayed calm in their room. I could be wrong, because if I even saw them they were fucked. Anyone I so much as looked at became instantly hammered—I was as drunk as five men and contagious. Had a good long chat with RJD about the state of things—about what to do when people throw shit at you (he says stop the show, I say throw it back), debated the matter for quite some time and what it comes down to is, he's Ronnie James Dio. The judges from the Miss America thing come along on account of my long-since-forgotten presence at their proceedings over an hour ago, with a video camera. They want explanations and the tapes, but I don't remember a thing. Turns out they're from New York. Drinks come, problem fades.

The OPEC guys are getting good and drunk by now, whooping their hats around. I was exquisitely moved by their table centerpiece—a two-hundred-dollar bottle of scotch—so I found myself segueing happily into a genuine conversation about logging futures. There was a long moment towards the end or the middle of the night when someone started *doing very bad things*—and everyone believes this absolutely to have been me—and that person had to be tossed into an elevator and sent back to the fifth floor for a little "time." Probably that person ran around the halls with his pants ankled yelling, "I am the Man on the Silver Mountain." And then probably fought his way back into the bar later. And maybe was seen later with a roadie humping a giant cooler filled with beers, spilling its contents all over the lobby with fanfare.

Sadly today the operation changed from search and rescue to recovery.

The next morning in the lobby doing the crossword or fuckwhatall, these moon-eyed Amazonian tweens are coming to me with glossy photos and two-one-two numbers and agency information, escorted by confused stage parents. I don't know what they're talking about. Then the oil barons, aiming their ten-gallon hats into the day's business, come with backslaps and secretaries' numbers in Houston and Kuwait. They're calling me by name, saying that was a "hoot" with the fire escape and where'd you get those watermelons? In the end, I wound up with a few nicknames I don't understand. When I went to retrieve my wallet back in the room, I found a watermelon in the tub.

The Warmth of Igloos

Lubbock, Tex.

The marquee on the club reads:

TONITE!

RONNIE JAMES DIO

WET T-SHIRT CONTEST

This will be a good show.

Asked Scott if the crew wants their cooler back now and where should I put it and he says, put it in your trailer and when it gets empty, we'll fill it with beer. He's not kidding.

Bachanailya
Big D

So this here would be the first arena we've ever played. The lineup is Dio, Sebastian Bach, Enuff Z'Nuff, and us; reverse order of course. LA Guns cancelled, but it sold out anyway. The first guy we run into is Paul Crook from all-time gracious tour hosts Anthrax. He is all smiles and remembers our names. Very pleasant. Maybe it was all just a bad dream. His new guitar is like a Jolly Rancher with strings. Now that he's being pleasant and social, we'd hang—but we gotta go sit in the lobby and wait for the limo. Really.

Had a bite to eat with Sebastian Bach in catering. That is a thing to do. He is constantly making as much noise as possible. He's whooshing around, bright yellow pants. He's lunging at the buffet with a bowie knife.

"Man, it was a fucking rip-off. We got paid eight hundred dollars for selling out the L.A. Forum. *Sold out!* You know how many people fit in the L.A. Forum? Well, *ppft*, a fucking lot. You don't make just. . . . hey! Hey, Bob! Get over here! Those posters come yet? Well, get 'em the fuck up, man! Jesus! *(Stabs a pepper)* Yeah, so fuck the Forum, man. And don't trust *anybody*, ever. Everybody's a fucken liar. What is this, tuna? Hey, 'scuse me, ma'am? This, right here, is this tuna?"

Mr. Bach is one of the lucky ones so far; he can still draw people into a room and remembers what to do when they get there. He's holding a roasted pepper on the end of a dagger while talking seriously about going Broadway. Seems to be faring pretty well, with his girlfriend managing him and "all you need is fans, man." True. Kind of. None of us remembered to ask him how it was with the Frogs. Busy just trying to keep the soup on the fork.

Enuff Z'Nuff used our equipment, which looked quite funny and was not enuff, and then they smoked something

with us later that turned me into a fucking cartoon. Everyone around became either an anvil with legs running
around or a hammer. Matt threw a pile of our "glossies" at
Steve for making us miss "Youth Gone Wild" (that *was* disappointing), nearly getting a busted nose in return. Coked-
up record people everywhere, and some other bullshit. You
know.

The Rape of the Locks

San Antonio, Tex.

Very much to our surprise, we are joined tonight by Budgie.
A band called Legs Diamond will be playing at some point.
They, according to *everyone*, are more popular than Led
Zeppelin in San Antonio. Officially.

Steve and I crashed the nearby Japanese gardens with
Foster's Oilcans, which we instantly drained and then
pissed out secretly behind some rice paper. The label rep is
utterly punctual and exceptionally helpful, rolling through
the place with a heap of well-mannered retail folk. Our
conjoined parties are engaged directly in a series of nearly
blinding contests of consumption. Budgie, it is pleasant to
note, are considerably more rock and roll than most bands
half their ages, so I collected some autographs on something which I lost thirty seconds later.

A Geographah at the Spowats Bah

The show, at a sports bar, had been very good and well-
wishing Texans approached us afterward. Texas is the best
place to play if you even *half* rock. One of our new friends
was curious about my accent. I am not aware that I have
one, but if I do, well, I would be curious to know about it,
too. I told him I was from New England. He looked sort of

blank for a beat, then with a big Texan grin and a back slap, "Well then, welcome to The U. S. of A!"

Winging It in Anytown

? – *U.S.A.*

Pain. In a room. Nothing familiar anywhere. Firm mattress, doilied bedspread. Mild alarm. Felt baseball pennants hanging on the wall. Model battleships on a desk. Tiny model crews spy through itty binoculars a recruit with fucked-up hair, whiskey damage and amnesia.

An old woman with a shiny walker hobbled past the doorframe, saying, "Farewell," with a little parade wave, "and Happy Easter." This was either meant for me, or for no one in particular, who is also me. Also, it wasn't Easter. While dressing clumsily, I noticed I was wearing a t-shirt with a kitten on it.

I walked into a kitchen. A family was there. A guy in his late teens in a backwards ball cap is over a pan of scrambled eggs. An older man is reading a newspaper. A young girl in pigtails is eating cereal. The kid at the stove goes, "Whoa! You're alive!"

"You sure?" I ask this fully allowing that the afterlife might be an infinity of Cleaver-esque breakfasts with total strangers. I sit in front of the selection of jams on the table, resolved to what, I don't know, but resolved. The little girl is looking at me with disinterest. Her lower jaw is barely clearing the table, and not at all when she chews. The newspaper man peers around the newspaper.

"Morning."

"Good morning."

Well, all right.

I realize that everyone, except for possibly the little girl, assumes that I am absolutely clear on my surroundings.

The chef unravels the fantastic and possibly true tale of how I came to be eating eggs in a family home in Smithville, Texas.

After breakfast, we're backing out of the driveway in the kid's Honda, so that I might be transported back to reality—or the other thing with the van and so forth. In a window, the old woman was waving, mouthing, "Happy Easter."

Fine. Happy Easter.

Top-floor hotel rock and roll shit after. I was face flat on the bed, supernaturally exhausted. A Flowbee model was on the phone ordering cocaine from her mother, who runs a delivery. Then it's dark. I must have passed out for a while, because there are more voices in the room, fading in and out. One keeps telling me over and over that "the eagle has landed."

Later on in the night, or maybe it was earlier, I walked into a pole and messed up my nose, but proceeded nonetheless into another of these "nightclubs" where I signed some posters for people who probably thought I was someone else. Ultimately, the night ends when Tim and I retire to the room to film things falling accidentally from the balcony. Then, at the outset of some new energizing late-night adventure, everything goes black again.

In the morning, we drive directly to a load-in dock just outside of Indianapolis, where there is a friendly leather security midget. He's got beer. There's an enormous guy near the midget, or rather, near the beer. Later, his buddy Bindle (yes, Bindle) pulls me out to the lot to tell me he has much to offer, but not in the way of the cocaine drugs that I had, for obvious reasons, expected. He's got "videos." He slips me a beeper number.

"So you're the . . . porn . . . man?"

He's completely taken aback. He clarifies in a long stoned drawl, "Noooo, duuuude. Meeetaaaal! I have *everything*."

Bindle unzips a duffel, and one by one pulls out the videotapes: Ozzy pushing Lemmy on a swing, a Stryper rehearsal, etc.

What.

Foil, hot dogs, a book, lighters, cans, a tennis ball; coins ricocheting off the amp grills; bananas, a stool, PVC tubing, a length of rebar (very bad), nachos, and a direct hit to the face with a hamburger. A light bulb, beef jerky, a boot, another boot, a shoe, batteries, screwdriver, a bottle, and throughout, the chant: *"Fuck You, Fuck You, Fuck You!"* Then, incredibly, a barrage of *full* cups of beer. For the Detroit audience, thirty-five-hundred-strong at the end of a long workday, it was more important to hate us than to *drink*.

"Who threw the *fucking* rebar? Who? What are you a fucking *psycho*?"

"*Fuck* you!"

Another hail of change. Another piece of construction material. The dark column was also managing to batter Dio's equipment. The crew is dragging amps and racks back into the right wing.

Then someone got the idea to light things on fire and throw them. Most of this doesn't quite reach the stage, or goes out, but there are a few successes. This needs to be stopped, but no one can, probably not even Dio at this point. It's a *situation* now. We had endured for quite some time, and although we were now engaged against the full wrath of Middle Earth, they had endured more. The place was oversold. Worse, doors had opened at five o'clock and people had begun arriving shortly thereafter. That factory whistle blew, and a thousand-plus fans beelined for Dio, some without going home to drop off their *tools* and other heavy projectiles. Metal videos projected onto the screen/ stage curtain were the only distraction as the room filled steadily for four hours. Four hours to drink and wait, pumped up by Motörhead videos and every half hour or so, a false alarm that Dio is about to deliver them. Metal longing is mounting. Pulling back a bit of the screen, currently at the outset of apparently a *very* popular Static-X video, there was barely time to take into full account how dangerous it looked out there before the screen began to rise. The retreating video screen received loud boos and it shivered from a bottle or two. Then it dawned on this desperate mass that Dio was upon them, and the place erupted ecstatically. Until the lights went up—not on Dio at all— but The Unband, who have chopless drinking songs.

Some places are easier than others to watch tourmates from the wings, and this theater, with direct bus-to-backstage access, was an easier one. So when the first bottle hit, Simon Wright, Jimmy Bain, and the techs were in the wings. By the end of the second song, the musical portion of the set was basically over. Ronnie James was by this time watching with concern. An award for best horrified expression goes to Chris the bass tech for looking as helpless as we should have felt. Instead, we were feeling *punk*.

"No *fucking* rebar!" This demand was met by more metal skidding across the stage. An empathetic couple at the front of the stage began rallying against the tide, prompting a bald maniac to *shove the woman*.

Leaping off the stage into the audience, swinging the bass. Receiving drunken blows, soaked, trapped, looking up at the stage: seven wet impossible feet away. Leapt, ten fingers from someone, pulled up by someone else. A plastic cup full of beer sailed over Eugene's drum set and landed on Simon Wright's.

As the screen dropped, the combined crews grabbed mops and shovels. A piece of rebar had come to rest an inch away from puncturing a speaker cone. A cup of beer stood on Simon's snare drum as if it had been set down gently instead of hurled with rage from the middle of a murderous horde. A solitary golden drop glistened in the center of the drumhead.

Dio.

10

Def Leppard Is Not the Luckiest Band in the World, Exactly

```
DEF LEPPARD/THE UNBAND
SUMMER TOUR 2000
```

First Leg

There is no question that having the run of an arena will be a thing. Quite possibly, it makes no sense at all. Of course, neither does anything else—and this is catered. And it's summertime, and the lawns will be smattered with people getting drunk on their quilt islands, all sausage grease and feeling each other up. Nice, like when they show *The Wizard of Oz* in the park.

We have more guys with us now, augmenting the well-soiled Machine that is Steve, Eugene, Matt, and myself: Safety-Bear very much comes from Vermont and is recently married. Steve performed the ceremony, having been ordained in some mail-order church just before a previous tour. Steve also gave Safety-Bear the nickname, for reasons which did not become clear until Safety-Bear later quit following some very unsafe behavior. He is handy with things and hammers, and is one of this planet's Nice Guys, as it were. Peeler is an ex-delinquent from Chicopee who can drive without sleep for days on end, tech the drums and, not least, is a crackerjack B & E man. Neither of them has been on a rock tour—or out of New England for any other reason—until now. Taylor has got a week or so off from a timelier sort of summer tour and is doing sound for the first few shows. No idea what we'll do about front of house after he leaves, but he's the only guy who's ever been able to mix us just right, and he's got some pills, I think.

We're traveling in two vehicles now. This one, a Dodge conversion van, used to be white and inconspicuous. Now it looks as if the shades are closed for a very good reason, which is nerve-wracking on the open highway because they *are* closed for a very good reason. The VCR's busted, but it's some comfort to have one. Ballast, like most of our amplifiers. All in all, considering what we put this van through, we can't complain, and there's a fairly good chance it'll make it through this tour. For some reason we have also a Ryder panel truck. I believe we were all under the impression that there was another van coming along, but I don't see one.

We also have acquired a, how would you say . . . giant hand. I can't recall whether it's a right hand or a left hand at the moment, but I know it's red and around eight feet tall inflated. We had it designed by some parade-balloon company in the Midwest. It was kind of a joke idea we mentioned at some kind of meeting at the label, then one day the fucking thing showed up. It grows out of a big black box when plugged in and you can make it sign any number of ways. We generally have it throw the goats. Obviously.

The "pyrotechnics" will probably be of use at these shows. The effect is achieved by taping fireworks to the instruments. We get them at this airplane hangar jammed with cheap explosives off of I-70 on the way to Chicago. All fireworks here are called things that have been translated from the Chinese: you have your Violence Ammunition, your Hard-Killing Mobster, your Disco Maimers and Explosion Face Policeman. Everything costs about fifty cents, and since we'll be playing outdoor places for the next few months, I brought along some extra Rape Volcanoes.

Every place on the itinerary is named after a soft drink or a computer company and frequently something worse. As right as it once seemed to complain about the Stones taking dirty beer money they didn't need, the phrase "Budweiser Presents" implies a certain kind of party that diarrhea medicine does not. Now it seems if you want to see anybody, you will see them at the Imodium Center and that's that. It's seven hours to Darien, New York—which is Rochester to some, Buffalo to others.

I-Am-a-Gettin'-It

Six Flags Amusement Park
The Something-Something Video Store Amphitheater
Darien, N.Y.?
7/22/00

Took a little something last night just as things were getting underway. Got through a glass of scotch and a glass of wine before passing out against the window. Woke up here, to roller coaster sounds: screaming, metal on metal. Parking lot has the four Def Leppard buses and two semis, our van and our mysterious panel truck, and a Free Beer and Canapés tent. We're parked behind the stage. Sixteen and a bit elephants could stand up there comfortably; this place holds twenty thousand something. For contrast, the last place we played was a sports bar on a stage that could fit possibly a lute, a midget and a plastic flamingo. If you had those.

Had a bit of breakfast (a nice peach and a teabag in a Chivas), read a magazine for a while, drank the last of the wine and went back to sleep in the van. Woke up around twelve-thirty. Ate a lunch of tuna salad, coffee, two beers, and watched the lighting guys swing around. It's all very impressive, but this is why people eventually start sticking fish into the groupie. Down time. Let's put this in a nice syringe, or how much will you give me if I get that chick to do this on that and then eat it? But it's all been done. We can be entertained by a much more wholesome enterprise: there's an amusement park ten feet from us. It will keep us occupied if we get high enough, and generally we do.

We were sitting around the sparse dressing trailer pacing around, and winding strings, and making little organizational lists (these will be lost right away, and by day three it won't matter). Joe Elliot came in. He warned us that though the weather looked okay right now, his band "wasn't the luckiest band in the world, exactly," and that it would probably rain for the rest of the tour. He then eyed our card table, on which was an allotment that ignored our rider completely unless there's a new one in which we ask for "jack shit."

Upon returning from some pharmaceutically haunted flume ride a short time later, it was obvious that Mr. Elliot had spoken with the catering bastards. The card table had been switched out for a solid dining one with a tablecloth and stocked with fruit, food, booze, and beer. And a table lamp.

Pyromania

Tweeter Center
Mansfield, Mass.

You would have to look a ways back, but our band is actually from Boston—and whatever is the opposite of the Key to the City, we have that. I remember being flung by giants into the Fenway while someone cursed me through a machine stuck into the hole in his throat. He tossed a red velvet jacket and a guitar cable after me. That was around seven years ago. This is as close geographically as we've come since then. Anyway, here are two catering tents, one with beer and one without. I was brought in a golf cart to the correct one about twenty minutes ago. Didn't see a single person until just now when Phil the guitar player came by to get more soy milk for the other tent. He apologized for our accommodations yesterday, and offered that if we ever find we need anything, we shouldn't hesitate to make it known. It's a cloudless eighty degrees, and so far each member of Def Leppard is easily as hospitable as a grandmother.

Our room is a locker room with leather couches, a clean carpet, and separate shower stalls. There's a lot of shrimp. Thanks to a very good friend/tireless supporter who is always showing up like a redemptive meteor when we're "tired," there is a supply of *wakey-wakey* in amounts befitting the auspicious occasion of our "finally making it"—in other words, an "assload." One bathroom is therefore off limits to everyone but the band and its tireless supporter. Matt's whole family is here, including a couple of cousins and the like. They all look confused and proud. Monahan is here, too: drinking fruit juice with no vodka in it, trying not to talk about his novel to the guy who's not doing the video. There are Northampton people along to help out (helping: guy offers to roadie and do lighting or "whatever"; gets a free ride here in lieu of an amplifier or a band member, some woman he wants to fuck gets guest-listed with her six friends, while the main guy drinks everything in sight, eats the dip with his hands, insults somebody's girlfriend, pisses off security, and passes out before we even load in). Old friends in various stages of liver failure are shotgunning a Bud suitcase every thirty minutes. The buffet looks less like it has been ravaged than like someone dropped a Buick through it.

Someone in the Leppard crew came in a while ago to ask the room if anyone wanted to put in an order for the "cigarette run," everybody piped up, and now the runner has returned with a carton of each brand and nobody has any money. So we're into the Leppard for a hundred something, and we have two cartons of so-and-so's fucking honey-nut-menthols eating up our per diems.

On the loading dock, we tried to get our fireworks bit okayed by Def Leppard's road management.

"So it'll just be that I light this fuse here . . ."

"And what happens, exactly?"

"Something."

"What do you mean. What is that thing?"

"It shoots fire."

"Uh huh. What kind of . . . *fire*?"

"Chinese. We get them at a place."

"You're fucking kidding, right?"

"Um. No."

"You aren't even really sure what that's gonna do. Are you?"

"It's okay. It's got duct tape on it. Watch."

The dock is showered by a twenty foot, totally uncontrollable arc of dime-store napalm, which immediately ignites a plastic No Smoking sign, curling it into a charred tube. The whole dock smells like shit. Some guy doing things with boxes down the end goes what the fuck.

"That looks like a 'No' face."

"Close. It's a 'No Way in Bloody Hell' face. And what exactly does this 'Hand' do again?"

Our attention is drawn to a treated rubber pad that

covers about ninety percent of the stage so that you're standing on a twenty-foot Def Leppard logo that prevents splinters and grounds your band in an electrical storm. They are very touchy about it because it cost eleventy billion dollars. "Nobody lights any fucking fires on this." They are watching. On the way out to soundcheck, I ran into Vivian Campbell and gave him a cheery greeting, but his face sank—later revealed to be due to the Rainbow tour shirt I was wearing. Everybody's got their *things*.

Absolutely high as jackasses when we get on stage and the crowd is silent. *Silent.* Every once in a while, someone way back on the lawn yells out "faggot!" The response to this is to single him out and then get the camera guy in the pit to put the guy up on the Jumbotron. The only time we got any applause was by arbitrarily shouting "Aerosmith!" Unless you count the horrified golf clap for "Everybody Wants You." Towards the middle of Def Leppard's set, during "Photograph," our friend from Hudson, Massachusetts, wandered obliterated from the dressing room out onto the stage trying to eat a mangled roast beef sandwich through his hair. Security, etc. As we were loading out, I saw a little bit of roast beef on one of the Leppard guitars.

Noted: Mansfield is a suburb of Framingham.

Foreshadow Puppets

Safety-Bear got us so stoned that we were able to make shadow puppets under a streetlamp in a rest area for hours. We had a bit of the vending, then drank a case-plus of leftover catering beer and argued about money, of which there is none. Van smells like absolute ass, so I took something and slept in the bushes.

Joe Elliot Had a Mott the Hoople Tattoo Before You Did

Jones Beach Amphitheater
Long Island, N.Y.

Today we were told some Rules. Behind *Behind The Music*.
Def Leppard are "cleaned up" now so we're not supposed to
be "drunk in catering," which seems impossible and is. Ian
Hunter came out and sang "All The Young Dudes" with
Leppard as an encore. Brilliantly. We met him in catering.
We were drunk. What.

Blossom Music Center
Cuyahoga Falls, Ohio
8/2/00

Sitting in a dressing room that looks like the common
room at a hippie college. Orange couches, white cement
walls, brown-grey lockers. Def Leppard is upstairs sound-
checking.

F-F-F-Foolin' . . .

I'm licking my finger to get the residue off of the table,
when I notice that the table covering and the cups and
plates are for a *Little Mermaid* birthday party. The Mermaid's got powder stains all over her face and she's been
anatomized with a sharpie.

Everyone is concerned that it makes no sense to be here.
Budgets and career moves are discussed. Quite diplomatic
and reasonable, the whole thing. Points are made. Not ugly,
exactly, but tense. Reminding anyone of anything that
anyone had been voicing daily while the idea of touring
with yet more metal bands in increasingly isolationist
venues is pointless. Look, what's done is done. You can't
dump off a high-profile tour that half the fucking people

we work with stuck their necks out for and go home and expect everyone to apologize. Eat your London broil and shut the fuck up. Points, however, have been made. Lessons will be applied in the future. Could be worse.

The huge hospitality room down the hall has a free video arcade which is entirely free, Ping-Pong and a putting green, a jukebox (also free for no money which is coincidentally how much I have), and huge windows looking into a dense elfin wood. It's like an abandoned Renaissance fair. All is well, but the food looks . . . I hear now behind me that there is some more residue left over from last night's atrocious binge. There'll be no bother about the wheat germ sloppy joes or "chili."

The Leppard guys were given this tiny gold circus motorcycle recently, I forget where. They each ride it around from time to time, but right now I'm watching Rick Allen, who is doing lazy figure eights out in the lot while smoking a cigarette and talking on a cellphone. Bike's gleaming, nearly blinding every time it passes the window. Replace the minibike with a drum set and you've got him at soundcheck too. I haven't quite figured him out: an optical illusion. It's not like everything around him is customized—just the drums. But he's so adapted that he appears less like he has one arm and more like he has three.

There is a parrot here who doesn't give a shit. He rides around on the shoulder of one of the Lep roadies. People give him grapes and such. He's frequently alone on one or other of the tables in catering with a paper plate of melon rinds in front of him, just thinking I guess. Right now he's sitting on the pinball machine. Thinking. I don't know what his name is. It is good to have a pet on the road—especially a wise-ass one with his head around things and some command of English.

During our set, three Def Leppards were laughing—at us

or with us, as usual it doesn't matter—in the wings while we played a Quiet Riot cover for eight thousand people. Joe Elliot, upon hearing us massacre it at soundcheck had specifically asked/dared us to play it. No one in the audience was laughing all that much. There were at least four hundred musical geniuses sitting there fuming, going "who the fuck are these assholes? I could fuckin' do that." Yes, but you're not.

The Ryder truck has disappeared and the rental van has showed up. It is immediately broken and sent to Assy McRipoff's Auto by Safety-Bear, who cannot hide the fact that he needs a break.

Possibly he is nervous about being lumped in with us, constantly in "trouble" with people. He probably hears what people say behind our backs, and I'm sure it's terrible shit.

So with only one vehicle now, we're fucked, but the Leppard crew offers some room and the most important things—the Hand, a couple of guitars, some leftover chicken—are put into their truck to be met at the next place.

Hey, How Come This Is Wet?

Let me say about how we urinate. We go and buy three gallons of water at a place that has a bathroom. We use that bathroom as much as we can after we have drunk as much of one of the gallons of water as possible. We put whatever is left into smaller containers, which we put somewhere in the van (gets nice and hot on those long desert drives), leaving half an inch of water in the gallon jug. Now this is a toilet, or more specifically, a urinal, and we use it when we're riding around. The brand we have now is called "Rock Spring Water." Any way you pair those words works. Especially "rock water." I used to sneak around when it was my turn to dump it. Now I just pour it out wherever I feel like and say, "What the fuck are you looking at?" The other gallon jug we dump out and fill with prostitutes.

Baptists

Gas Station—Somewhere in Missouri

Safety-Bear opens the driver's side door and a few Budweiser bottles roll out and smash on the ground. Matt is throwing up out the back of the van. A jug of piss is leaking toward our neighbor's car; the guy's got one hand on the pump and an expression on his face that defies description—wait, no it doesn't—it's fear and disgust. Inside the store, I've knocked over a rack of something blurry. Steve is paying for some Big League Chew with his pants down. His raspberry-glass KISS belt buckle scrapes along the linoleum as he walks out.

The only person who isn't frozen is a giant woman tending to a nacho accident all over the counter. She's using a magazine to shovel cheese-food back into its pan under the heat lamp in one of the most retarded operations I have ever witnessed. She says, "There must be a better way to do this, but Baptists don't know it."

Additionally, today was Joe Elliot's birthday. We gave him a *Boy Scout Handbook*, copyright 1948, and a stickpin that says "New England: Caring Is Our Way."

Now I'm shotgun in the van back on the highway. Listening to some Mountain. It is proud, proud music.

Winks

Slept sitting up in a rest area again. As a matter of fact, from now on, that goes without saying. I owe any moments of blissful unconsciousness to lots of booze and pills and wine—the same goes for consciousness, I guess. Tylenol PM works only about twenty-five percent of the time now. "Sleep" almost always means pass out cold, "tired" means walking coma, "take a nap" means suddenly collapsed in the middle of something. And so on. The place we played last night was called the Smirnoff Center. Or if it wasn't, it certainly is now. So I slept some.

Driving. There is a terrible song on the radio. We can only listen to the radio a couple hours per day because the van's electric is shot and we can only afford batteries for the portable once a week. Battery time is much better spent on talk radio or, say, white noise. Except in Ohio. There's good radio all over the place there. Makes you wonder who knows anything about anything.

King of the Naptime World

No one on the planet can sleep like Eugene Ferrari. Four-teen hours and counting, with his jacket on in the chair. It is 113 degrees today. We're coming up on Little Rock, Arkansas.

Hail to the Pimp

Little Rock. This is by far the hottest the world has ever been since its oceans were lava. The Heat Index is one hundred and seventeen, and at some point we will get under the gazillion-watt stage lights. People are frying eggs on everything. It's hard to breathe.

Across the park is a "discovery store" for kids. It's cooled by NASA or some god-machine from the future, so I spend several hours discovering shit. Bug Boxes. Solar Kites. Phantom of the Opera chemistry sets. A good many of the things to discover involve Bill Clinton in some way: cutout fashion books, *What Does the President Do All Day* pop-up book, etc. They've got Hillary looking a lot like Sharon Stone, and Bill looks like Superman's more ass-kicking brother. Which, by the way, he is.

Catering was hilarious today, unless you're starving of course. The macaroni was with hot dog bits and the pound-cake squares had food-coloring designs on them that have run in the heat so that each piece looks like it says "die" in pink. I don't know what it said before. A lunch-lady asked a four-hundred-pound local stagehand if he was a vegetarian as he stood there with two chops and a burger on his plate. He said, "Yes, ma'am!" so she lumped him some collards. An old guy brought our beer to us in a mop bucket along with our package of Oscar Mayer and some grapes. The Def Leppard gentlemen live in castles, and I've seen their cart— they're not faring much better. I do not wonder why there are sweaty envoys from the local food shacks going in and out of the dressing rooms. Even catering got a few pizzas brought in.

Stage set was stripped down because the stage is a little smaller (though the venue was basically the entire river-front with people spilling back into the streets and watching from rooftops—a *lot* of people). There was no rubber mat thing that nobody lights any fires on, and I missed it because my whole body is like Hellraiser with splinters from the stage. One went practically through my kneecap. They tried to keep the lights down a little, but when the spots hit you, you're an ant under a magnifying glass. Matt introduced "Everybody Wants You" as a song "penned by Mr. William Squire." Blank stares and total silence. Then, "Umm . . . . *Billy* Squire", and the place went nuts.

The bar five minutes away is open until 5:00 A.M. for regular people and then later for people on rock tours. Couldn't keep my eyes open at just past three-thirty. Steve became something from redneck mythology, as he is wont to do, though this was very unusually inside of four beers. We were all just that spent. He was just about to rock the place with the chair over his head when I took a nap.

Matt wins the prize though: a Christian librarian and her mute and even more Christian friend followed him from our show, tagging very quietly along not drinking, watching him booze like a Hun—I don't know if he even tried to talk to them at all after the Lord came up during initial back-stage conversation. To their credit, they sat calmly and patiently on a bench in Sodom as if they were waiting for a bus. Finally in the wee-wee hours, these girls were seen sitting on either side of him with their hands folded in their laps. He was swaying on the bench having no idea where he was. Then he face-planted on the table and started snoring. He was soon carried out as the girls looked on not saying anything, not drinking, hands folded—left behind in a place where at 5:00 A.M., someone was screaming for body shots. I don't know what became of those Christians. Off to not drink somewhere else, I suppose. It's incredible how many people just pass through your life once for a minute or two.

I don't know if I was helping to carry someone or if I was being carried myself, but everybody flung everybody else into the van, and we were off to a rest area somewhere not far.

Last gig on this leg is tonight. Then we hit clubs for a couple weeks and hook back up on the West Coast for another month of dates with the Brits. Don't know where exactly we're going next, but it better not be western Pennsylvania. We're at the Hair Club for Men Amphitheater. It has a small, stagnant pond behind it with a putting green floating in the middle. There are a few beavers, some frogs;

Cat-o-Nine tails sway around it. When you're eight, you smoke your first cigarette there. There's a little metal rowboat sitting on the bank. This is noticed and beverages are fetched from the van.

Steve, Safety-Bear, and I drain the boat and push it out on the pond. We're rowing around sipping Budweisers. We noticed a few huge buzzards circling above the arena. (When I mentioned this to Joe Elliot a little later, he laughed nervously.) Suddenly, there's ten thousand shit-fits coming from the shore. The place goes upside down. "YOU FUCKING DEAD FUCKING ASSHOLES! YOU PSYCHOTIC FUCKING BAGS OF SHIT! THE SHERIFF FUCKING BLAH BLAH BLAH!" And so on. At some point during the row back, Safety-Bear points out that these people are screaming at, for some confounding reason, the Artist. This upon reflection would serve to illustrate the difference between *Artist* and *Opening Artist*.

When we get back to the shore, there are maybe six fat guys shaking their drumstick fists at us. Hemorrhaging motherfuckers everywhere. Def Leppard's Tour Manager starts in with the "and another thing, that time you did this, and another thing, and what was that crap in such and such a place, and another thing about the dressing rooms, and who do you think you are?" As if we knew. This between bursts from the local guys about the "sheriff" and the "county lockup." Apparently, Andy Griffith is gonna work us over with a broomstick until the real police get there.

"Well, *Sirs*, we just woke up and were trying to have a beer in a boat like a *human*," and I'm about to get into it with where they can stick their liabilities and that festering ponds are my alma mater goddamn it, and I grew up on the water and I was out ramming sunfishes and pirating commuter boats while you were hanging out in a basement and *I* will tell *you* about the drinking in the boats. But then we learn that one of the guys had just pulled a body out of the pond last week following Ozzfest, so the place is a little sensitive to our kind of recreation. We didn't know this, and now we've Ruined Everything with our Cruel Prank.

Show went well and afterward there was an extra case of beer and a bottle of Ketel in the dressing room, so it seems we're okay. Backstage was unusually crowded, a little extra party in the open air to celebrate the switch to State Fairs. Joe Elliot came over to where Matthew and I were getting fucked up out of our skulls. He broke the ice with "Ahoy!" having heard about the rowboat debacle.

We asked him how he felt about playing the hayride circuit. Answer: "Excellent. People that go to those things bought a lot of our records," so playing some free shows was only right; and besides, "it's all rock and roll."

Here Comes the Colonel

We thumped across the infield of a greyhound track in Spokane right on time. A stage was being built to specifications that would dwarf all the other stages that we had been on during the past few weeks. Huge catering tents were being set up. We ghost-rode the van and tore out towards them. Chili. Beer. Shelter. A parrot. Freedom. Home.

For the first time, it occurred to us to have a full rehearsal—there was so much space. We asked for this, expecting nothing. Instead of nothing, several Leppard crew and some local employees took some time to clear out a storage garage by the access gate and rigged it with a generator. We tried unsuccessfully to get a Def Leppard cover together. Eventually, this turned into a small show for staff. One guy had parked his forklift and was leaning on the steering wheel.

After the show, we were as usual packed up by assistant promoters and brought to a gentleman's club. This one looked very exclusive. Very exclusive indeed—*devoid* of patronage, in fact. But it was offered to us by a person in a tuxedo. Everything at the bar would be gratis, as much as we could handle. As much *orange juice* and *ice cream* as we could handle—which is none.

"Look, not to be ungrateful, but do you think you might be able to show us something more . . . *disreputable?*"

Why Fences

A crackhead walks in the dressing room—as they do. No idea how this one got in, but he seems nice enough.

"So, man, so like, what's it like tourin' with Journey?" he says, snatching a sandwich.

Excellent. We clear some newspapers from the couch and give him a beer. He is provided a backstage pass and welcomed effusively. Maybe later he can meet Journey.

It's a good stage here because there's this sturdy looking bar-thing a few feet above and to the side of it. Looks like if you hit it right, you might be able to swing over the chain-link onto the lawn seats . . . fast forward: you can.

The grass was pretty filled in with people, and the second I cleared the fence onto their side they all started running—*booking* for the back wall. One woman, rather a larger sort, standing in front of me with her arms over her head, is screaming "No!!" Try to calm her down a bit, convince her that I'm not going to hurt her. It just gets worse, with me pointing to my bass, which is barely recognizable as a musical instrument anyway, and is currently spewing green smoke like a weapon from Jupiter. I think I'm helping, saying, "Where's your husband! Where's your husband!" (I had no idea where I was going with that.) I'm covered in drug sweat and have a gash on my head that's been bleeding so hard it's making a *sound* (I hadn't noticed this). For everyone's sake, I have to get back to the stage. As I'm making for it, all I can see is a maze of fences and confused security guards. I opt to toe up the fence on a mad run; hit the top and flip over violently, bounce my face off the other side of the fence, somersault down a small hill onto the concrete, and slam into the crowd barrier.

Had a quick party backstage with some Idaho people. Idaho people have been toying with genetics. The promoter's assistant had given passes to a troop of nice Boise girls. They have never in their lives been in the presence of anyone who has been to New York. They are peering at us uncomfortably from behind the crackhead. At one point, he nearly had them all in the sack with a story about his buddy getting his arm severed by a tractor, wrapped up nicely with a little wave from the other side of the room by a guy with one arm. A couple of wonderful persons have made their way to the backstage platter to fill their pockets with hummus. Everyone is the same.

Would have liked to go out on the town, or whatever they have here, but we've got to be in Vegas yesterday.

The Curse of Peter Lawford

There's no show here. Apparently there never was. We tried to drum one up, but somebody's holding a magnet under that roulette wheel. We have to wait for money from somewhere, as we are out of gas. At least we're in Vegas. This consoles no one, though I pretend some.

The motel is next to the Riviera. It's called the Tawdry Duke or something, or is at least decorated like it is. The hallways are red, with paintings of playing-card jacks and flickering electric lamps. A plastic chandelier hangs in the vending area, and by its light I can see that there is a greasy bag of peanuts midway off its balcony in the machine. Despite a substantial kicking and jostling, it remains there, insolent and unaffordable. Things are not good.

The room looks like a stuck conveyor in a slaughterhouse. I'm in the corner squeezing a relish packet into my mouth, the only food in two days. No one has said a word for over eight hours. We are at a crossroads. I'm going out.

Las Vegas will buy you drinks even at the five-cent slots. If you don't care about winning friends or taking home the waitress, you can maybe get trashed for a nickel, and I know I saw a nickel in the van. I searched, found the nickel, spit-shined it, put it in my pocket and headed for the casino.

My waitress was attentive as I picnicked on Chivas for two hours. Managed to get a bit of a buzz on, but couldn't find my room key so I slept on top of the van. Fell asleep thinking about slots . . . now *there's* a monkey on your back.

Through the Booking Glass, Darkly

L.A., Calif.

We are saved because our friend Mark has managed to get himself situated in a house in the Hollywood Hills, the actual kind: a view on three sides, one of which peers into the courtyard of a famous director's home. The garden path led to the hot tub. The house itself had a marble shower (and marble *countertops*), a fireplace, a turntable and a thousand records, an astounding Dutch hi-fi and ten thousand CDs, a good kitchen, and a very dangerous guestbook. There is some spare room, and it looks like we might be around for a while—no gigs scheduled for at least a week. But we *have* to ration the money to a depression-era extreme just to have gas to go to the next place.

Though there was no scheduled show, a long-shot call to the Whisky proved not only fortuitous (we got a slot) but serendipitous (The Eleventh-Hour Accomodating Fu Manchu were on the bill along with Supagroup, thickly rumored to rock). It was good for our spirits.

The Whisky was good that night, on the dark balcony especially. The show being a success all around, The Sensibly Booked Fu Manchu were off to Japan and Australia, and ourselves and the very Supagroup were off to the house in the Hills for just the rock-and-roll party you would imagine, if you could imagine it.

Virginia Beach
9/23

As I was eating crab legs today, a Honda went off the top floor of the parking garage across the street, landing between a Ferris wheel and the trailers that house the Budweiser Clydesdales. Check please, as they say.

The sun hasn't been out for a few days, and it's cold. Apparently we have *not* heard back from Matt, MIA for two days, so another show has been scrapped. Considered doing it anyway, just bass and drums. Isn't that a kind of music now, "bass and drum?" We never should have let him go back to New York. Back tomorrow. Right. Hopefully, this is not the end of the tour for us, but it looks bad.

Use the time to do some interviews for the Canadian thing. They're running some sort of contest where the fans (fans?) are going to choose a Canadian song for us to cover, for something. I say "These Eyes," or some April Wine, but this doesn't matter. I bet that never happens anyway. I have a good view of a very angry ocean right now.

9/24

Sun came out today. Crab legs. No show.

9/25

No sun today. Crab legs. No show.

9/26

Uh.

9/27

Partly sunny. Half full, whatever. The *Virginian-Pilot* wonders (and it was a Honda, mind you, not a *tank*) "whether the parking structure meets building codes." There is an investigation, but I can tell you right now. *No.*

We were going to try and make tonight's show, in somewhere, but Matt got on a train *this morning*, to come back *here*, apparently. And so that's it.

We'll go see Def Leppard anyway, and apologize. Bring them some booze or something. Or no. Something.* Kind of wanted to go to the fair anyway. They have the world's largest kielbasa there. Well, that's what they think.

*We brought maple syrup from our General Store, in bottles that look like Southern Comfort bottles. I stashed them in the catering tent during the show, and when I went back to retrieve them to give Def Leppard their parting gifts, they had been stolen, obviously by people who thought it was booze. Hey you: Surprise.

Part III

The End

II

Headstones and Halos

**THE HEADSTONES
&
THE UNBAND
CANADA OCT.–NOV. 2000**

*For a moment we glance back over the bayonet at
the gleaming road with its traffic and its people
strolling, freely, in a world that we have quitted.*

—*T. E. Lawrence,* **The Mint**

The thing with a time bomb is that the inevitable explosion doesn't matter—you go off in a million directions none the wiser. That's not what gets you. It's the goddamn *ticking.* And I don't remember much, but I know how it probably went: Creep up to the border in our Christmas sweaters, hands folded, teeth brushed, papers in order, a small pharmacy up our asses. Then comes a little professional chitchat about importing fruits and things with the customs people who, impossibly, don't perfectly get it that inside of twenty-four hours, we become a giant cauldron of drugs and filth—a windowless tower of consumption.

Anyway Toronto is just peeling itself open, the sun is limping out from, I imagine, its crappy hotel. We're just *elated* to be back in Canada.

Tick, tick, tick.

The Border

Eleven hours behind schedule—give or take a couple hours or so. The van is crammed with equipment, most notably a Giant Inflatable Hand for the making of giant inflatable gestures. We are shoehorned in, crushed and twisted between dilapidated amplifiers. Some kind of fluid is seeping up through the floor, smelling dangerous. We have something to drink.

Hit the border at around five in the morning. I had actually managed to sleep quite comfortably by dislocating my shoulder, removing one leg, breaking my own jaw, and curling up around the wheel well. I have photographs of the way Eugene was sleeping that make a yogi wince. Matt smells of vodka. Not like you do, but like a five-hundred-pound unemployed Russian does. Can't be one hundred percent on making it across. Maybe he could at least say, "I have nothing to declare but my shitfacedness," and we could go home happy. We're sent into the thing and greeted by a body builder reading a muscle magazine, who appears to be a Canadian off the boat, and by that I mean of course having that neutral charm that arises from having complete trust in the world and everything in it. Very nice for us.

It's been a week since we last took a mind-altering amount of cocaine. And it's been a long week. So long in fact that we might consider it to be three weeks, and so are congratulating ourselves on our restraint as we're leaning on the specked Formica at this customs hang, trying not to fit any profiles. One would think we were giving a flawless performance. Maybe they think we have money—I suppose we have almost twice as much as we do. The short of it is that more than likely, to the trained eye, we looked like a bunch of giant lizards in sombreros dancing around with kilos of things. Maybe we're getting good at this, but somehow they let us through. We could have smuggled in a god-damn elephant, but we didn't. We have an elephant guy in Ottawa, and that's the first stop.

Brothers in Harms

The Headstones are probably the best rock band we could possibly tour with right now because: a) they are very good, b) they are excellent people, and c) they are knowledgeable and accommodating in matters of internal *strife*. Is not talking or looking at each other for two weeks strife? Anyway, morale bad. Who would have thought? It seems so simple: here's some money, here's a tour bus, go play. It's not. It's not simple at all.

Anyway

Canadian bands are different. One reason is that they are Canadian. Another reason is that Canada is huge, and frozen all over the place. The idea of traveling up here, in the sense of a national tour, keeps me awake at night. If American bands were required to do this, there'd be about three. And they would probably all have Ian MacKaye or Henry Rollins in them. Drunks cannot do it, and we work *drunk*.

I have a recurring nightmare about touring up here—we have to do it in Eugene's old Volvo. The dominant feature of that car—that it had no floor—was a true and unique benefit in the summer. You didn't have to stop to go to the bathroom, a boon for a less-than-punctual rock band. And in the heat, you'd get a breeze (a little dirty maybe) or a cool refreshing spray off the road. But in the winter it was not so pleasant a touring vehicle. We made a few runs back and forth to the Berkshires that I remember in particular. Our equipment was bungeed to the backseat and I was straddling the speeding black void between the axle hump and the inch of space under the door, being pummeled with wind sleet and road slush for two hours. I dream terribly of making the Winnipeg-to-Vancouver run the same way. Then I wake in a bunk on a bus with food and television and whiskey and everything else.

Brandon, Manitoba

All the hours here hauling through the blizzard felt like being curled. Two caribou with giant brushes skated along ahead of the bus. Our destination was named like a cut-rate motel, but I imagined that it would be a club or theater. Nope. Stage is off the lobby. Strange, but incredibly convenient. The stage is a hallway away from sleep. Or rooms, anyway.

I am fading into the false grain of this paperboard desk, becoming quickly extinct, and not smoking about it. We played a campus nacho joint last night and a cold, nacho-less cattle hall the night before. I was envisioning the bus somersaulting across the tundra and skidding into a silo.

I should mention that this motel, I do not fucking know why at all, has a full-size waterslide into a pool that is at most three feet deep. You get smashed on the bottom and nearly die every time you slide. I hear. Similarly useless are the slot machines in the bar which do not under any circumstances give money or tokens or anything redeemable for anything.

Canada.

There is no reason whatsoever to go outside, where snow is piling up, the wind is very bitter, and there is nothing, nothing, nothing to do.

All figures in CAD:

Television	$200
Thermostat	$12.79
Assorted bedding	$45
Mirror	$62.50
Carpet cleaning	$59.95
Electrical	$75
Paint	$16
Replastering	$19
Framed Print: *Snowy Cabin, Lonely Duck*	$23.50
Peephole	$3.67

The act of trashing a motel room is wholly rational—and innate. The first strokes come long *after* reasoning, not before it. Most everyone, when put into a motel room, will get on the bed and watch television. The addition of a 9-iron and a pile of drugs will most of the time produce an equally universal activity. This sort of thing is about simple anatomy. You just take all the drugs and drink everything. That'll do the physical work. Now you are the coyote. Now you are the black bear. Your watching-self hangs above in ghostly peace as your throwing-self tosses the TV out the window. Since we were monkeys, we all knew how to do this. It is the Obelisk. Your grandmother or your cousin's baby could capably trash a hotel room if you got them just right in the thalamus. Of course, in the end, the reward is you sleep on glass and talk to cops, and somebody maybe takes all your liquor money for a week. And more unfortunately, this—like everything else—has been Done, and probably done better. Come to think of it, it should be that the Bonham and Moon estates set up a fund of some kind.

At any rate, the anatomy of this kind of evening itself is also simple: You have a room, supposedly for free and not in your name in a far-flung foreign hamlet where everything looks like a toy. You have a reserve of seventy-five drink tickets (I am not kidding about this at all), the usual powders, and a sack of mystery pills. Everyone is tired, drunk, horny, half-crazy, and furthermore have been given the run of the place because, though no one has any real idea who they are and they have absolutely no money, they are almost famous. No one sees a damn thing wrong with taking handfuls of something a toothless parolee is handing out in a bathroom stall, so there's nothing to be done, and pretty soon it's light-bulb baseball, lamp jousts, and ambulances.

We finish playing the gig, I retire to my room to shower, shave, bandage, check the messages, and huff a bit of what someone has told me is ether. Some minutes later, I'm coming back into the bar in time to see our tour manager tossing a table onto a heap of petrified waitresses. He is screaming. I can't tell what it is he is doing exactly, beyond what I can compare to a documentary I once saw about baboons. It had footage of the alpha male standing on a high jagged mountain ledge screaming the most incredible three-pitched banshee scream in natural history, one hand hurling boulders down onto the already half-devastated monkey kampong and the other with a choke-hold on his *murderous* purple hard-on. Matt, more subdued, is on the floor in a giant fur coat and a helmet rolling around knocking into things with his hand in his pants and yelling that he is being raped. He is "partying."

At a glance, this could be the spoils of tequila: I used to have a hippie come to my apartment in the mornings to try and stop my back from spasming enough so that I could get out of bed, and he was able to tell what I had been drinking the night before by pressing a certain spot on my heel. He would touch his thumb on my foot for just a second and say, "Jaegermeister." A similar kind of divination comes from looking at the structural damage to, say, a waitress station. Tequila alone does not normally—in our immediate circle, anyway—induce this kind of bug-eyed drooling and the laughing and crying at the same time with the pants down. Nobody anywhere has PCP, and we are not an acid crowd, so if one had to venture a guess, some mushrooms might raise their little hands. They grow all over the place around here, I remember being told, which explains a lot. At any rate, even through the haze of what someone told me is ether, it is clear that everything is going to come all the way fucking down.

So I settle in to watch a bit. Better yet, head back for the video camera.

Money Can Do Anything

Vancouver, B.C.

Lenny showed up today. It seems they've added a band that he's signing to the bill. I bet they sound like *something meets something*. We're going to go out to their parents' house later. It's an odd thing to do on the road—shocking, in fact: parents. We rolled the tour bus into a gated community in "cowtown" for a home-cooked meal. Astronauts, when they return to earth, decompress for *days* before they go to parents' houses, and they're not shoving speed into their eyeballs every five minutes. Or maybe they are.

Limo to suburbia. Families are nice. In Canada, they have ketchup chips.

Creeping Death

On the bus just now, we had yet another fucking mind-raping blowout over money. Matt seems to think you don't need to pay for things except beer. It boggles. He kept asking, accusing, what were these "hidden expenses" I keep talking about, when what I said was "unforeseen expenses." As in . . . When certain people fucking do hundreds of dollars of damage to hotels it comes out of the budget. When the amps blow up, it comes out of the budget. When dates get added, and you have to pay for extra days on the bus. The fucking books are wide open. Don't ask me where the money went—look in the fucking book. Gas, bus drivers, sound men, hotels, motels, overtipped strippers, drugs, T-shirts, posters, CDs, all of it. And frankly, in spite of all the bullshit, we're miraculously close to being on budget. It's just that *there isn't any money.* Riding on a tour bus doesn't mean *shit*—except that someone somewhere maybe thinks you can make back the gargantuan sums you are hemorrhaging every day. Look here, on the paper I can show you. Oh? Don't show you any of that bullshit, it just confuses you more? Everything: circular argument. The whole nasty business went on for far too long, with Lexi filming, and Steve not taking sides, which he thinks for some reason helps even when one person is doing his best not to complain while the whole fucking ship is going down, while another guy sits there drinking a Budweiser in *Canada* and calls his best friend of fifteen years a thief because he can't remember where he spent his per diem, and furthermore insists—on the advice of a woman who *aspires* to be Nancy Spungen, both of them navigating solely by the light of so many burning bridges—*insists* that we stop, quit the tour, split the money now, and that *he* will drive the bus the 2,496 miles—(pardon) the 3,906 kilometers—back to New York.

Things are not good. They will get worse.

I walked to the Sushi place and smoked a horrible Export A on the balcony with cold sake, and the empty boats went around and I mourned our band.

Eug, wisely, took evasive measures when the interviewer walked into the dressing room at the Commodore. Matt and I traded insults for twenty minutes until the interview kid was uncomfortable enough to leave. Big fan, he had said when he came in. Probably not anymore.

Headstones have stepped off the wagon, quite bravely. Unless I'm not supposed to say that, in which case everyone is fine and having a mocktail. Big all-star ending, with the hand flipping the "bird" for a change. I think we did "Stepping Stone." Backstage is tremendous.

Dear Abby,

Matt kicked me with his big steel-toed boot in the middle of the set (I'm in a disintegrating rock band called The Holy Terrors—our album is called *Everyone Is Fine and Having a Mocktail*, and is in heavy rotation on Radio Disney. In case you were wondering. *Wink wink. PLUG*.) Seriously, what should I do? I took some aspirin (if you know what I mean), but I'm running out of fucking cheeks to turn here. Wait. Are you *dead*? I forget.

Please write and let me know,

Busted On A Bus

Worse

At the last motel, Steve took us aside one at a time in his room to tell us that the van—the vansion, the vangina, our bread and butter—while being driven by a person by some stretch of the imagination in the employ of the band, was in an accident. This was a month ago. It's been in a disreputable-sounding private shop in upstate New York accruing fees since. Oh, and we owe the State of New York a couple grand in damages for the guardrail, and the person who drove the van was just diagnosed with the rapid onset of something terminal and only has a few weeks to live. So . . . there's that.

The van, however, was no problem. We'd have it back before we knew it.*

The Borderline

Duty Free. Salmon, and more salmon. Ice wine. I suppose one could spend one's tax refund stocking up on Absolut. After all, it is a whole *two* dollars cheaper.

Oh, look. A case of vodka.

Bad sign.

Auld Lang Shut the Fuck Up

New Year's. Back to Toronto through fifteen-hour blizzard, Eug drove, plowed through, incredibly. Puss and *ahem* are coming from the Maritimes, where they have been mincing around galleries and frolicking with picnic baskets. In the *pansies*.

Strange hotel—like a hostel. Separate rooms because people. A hostile.

---

*Gone forever.

1/1/01

El Mocambo. Band called Hot Piss. Dress as pharaohs. Very funny. Missed "countdown" event on stage, thank God.

Went to usual secret boozecan, forgot password. They let me in anyway. Too bad. Smell now, shit-feeling, no loonies for soup. Bovine Sex Club tonight.

1/02/01
5:00 A.M.

Bovine show was two hours straight, improvised most, some AC/DC, no words exchanged with singer.

Other than that, it was quite a good show I think, right Mrs. Lincoln?

Hey You! Dog Is Man Best Friend! Today Is Fine Day. Let's Go Out With Us!*

Chinatown here is better than in New York, or anywhere. I have become hooked on these little Listerine strips that dissolve on your tongue. I put whole packs at once. Sometimes two, to feel that.

Quiet at hostile. Everyone sleeps. How?

Watched another nature show with the sound low while everyone else in the room slept. A snake ate all his and his mate's eggs while she was out doing something. Then he left by means of *lateral undulation*. She should have stayed home; snakes around.

Of course, now there's nothing to worry about.

You Got Another Drink Coming

I do not by any stretch mean to suggest here, or anywhere, that we weren't all fucked up in one way or another. As an

---

*Ad copy for cellphone accessory.

organism, we were sick, dying. The malignancy was not getting a lot of immuno-defensive help. We were tired and had developed stress disorders, and there was no break ahead, no time to cool off. The cheapening outlives all; fueled on demise, it would go to work on legacy. And then it doesn't matter from what cave it crawled out, or who said what, or who did what. You blew it and you're done and it's over and that's it.

The Rapist

A plan was hatched between the record label and other concerned parties to get the band into group therapy, and incredibly, there was not much more than a little apprehension at first.

Matt's response was to suggest that we see a business manager instead, like he'd (quote-unquote) been saying forever. He had missed four meetings with one such person and three with another. We had missed them all too, having made a retarded pact that fiscal matters would only be discussed in the presence of all three idiots. Secretaries closed the datebook as soon as they heard my voice. We were casually blacklisted at several prominent firms. So if meeting a business manager was an uproarious joke of an expectation, a therapist was right out—even if he *had* fixed Aerosmith. We wouldn't be able to handle the soaring ballads, anyway.

Rehearsals were a necessary evil, and we necessarily avoided them nearly altogether as we prepared for another record. The riffs were still coming, but frequently they would be indistinguishable. The subject matter had become distinctly non-celebratory, ugly even. There was a little too much information behind too thin a veil of A chords.

The Ranch

Then, still on the label dime, we were sent out to the Woodstock area to do some recording at an old converted saloon. We brought forty bottles of wine and a pound of marijuana. The place had a great deal to recommend it, and we stayed for quite a while, sitting by the wood stove, sleeping, and staring at horses in the snow. It was good for that. But the most we did there was drink the wine in three days, become obsessed with taking ecstasy (therapeutically, of course), and turn an entire corner of the kitchen into a gravity bong. Two weeks later, there were a couple toss-off cover songs and a few long electric piano solos.

Running Out the Tank

Mistress Cute-as-a-Button used to say that our band wore a halo of blood. I always found that a bit morbid for our style, but the point was taken. The band has always been protected by the more mysterious aspect of the same reckless stupidity that keeps us in harm's way. Our successes live behind a door to which folly is the key. We should be dead, or at least hospitalized more frequently. Certainly we should have been dropped by our label with extreme prejudice. Yet we were headed out on another tour.

```
┌─────────────────────────────────┐
│   THE UNBAND/ BLACK HALOS       │
│        East Coast Tour          │
│          Spring '01             │
└─────────────────────────────────┘
```

Cigarettes

Philly

No girls allowed in dressing room. Good rule. We will make it when it *suits* us, thank you. Girls in dressing room. I need a cigarette. Fuck, quit.

I'm having a cigarette.

The Black Halos are young, in leather. They think they are the Dead Boys or something, but it's more like they're a competent Germs. Which, in this day and age, is better.

Booking weenies didn't pay. Offered instead to lock the door after the show, and "give us a few on the house." *Whaddaya say, buddy!* Like that, like a car salesman. Biggest fucking mistake he'll make this year, besides inviting us back in advance.

After only a few drinks, he asked us if we thought we could convince Sebadoh to play his club, with *his* band. We said sure—but it's going to cost you.

I got on the bar phone to the Bombay Hilton.

"Hey, Jason, how are you? What? Bah. You want to play with a Limp Bizkit–influenced fusion band at the place they don't pay you in Philly?"

An Indian bellhop repeated, "Excuse me, this is Bombay Hilton." I put him on hold, we drank.

New York

Everybody. Blow.

Boston
The Compound
Williamsburg, Mass.

Took the dogs to the vet today. Greyhounds' teeth are more expensive than Old Dirty Bastard's. Less bling except for the Keek, who needed a new rhinestone collar for the party. Kiki had all but eight of her teeth removed and the same went for the Professor. He, however, is amusingly unused to sedatives and slumped against the counter at the post office like a drunk. I ran a stamp for the oil bill along his lolling tongue. I was sending a bad check and would be in court presently.

Went to the town meeting regarding the library renovation funds. An unsightly portion of the town was *extremely* uncomfortable with the idea of more books. There was a close vote, ending in favor of *not* reading and allowing children Kipling only with the dark people crossed out.

The Halos called to say hello after the show we should have been playing. Nobility, unity—things we once knew. We were thankful and promised to at least attend the next show. We didn't talk long because we had to get to the party.

Everyone who was anyone was at the party: Eugene, myself, a giant bottle of scotch, and let's see . . . that's all. The party was a great success.

Portland, Me.

N.H. State Liquor Store.
Portland is good. Kids are fucking mad for it up here. The Skinny. Must send them a card. The Black Halos were on tonight. Watched from stage scaffold. Got fucking *whacked* afterwards with local kids. One more show, then taking a *fucking* break. See about this book business.

On Shutting the Barn Door After the Horses Are Dead

Bowery Ballroom, New York
7/29/01
Heroin Sheiks, The Unband,
Interpol, Udet

We arrived very separately at the Bowery. "That's good enough," I said at soundcheck when it wasn't even close to passable. The monitor guy, a total stranger, put his hand on my shoulder and said he was sorry, and that it had been hard to watch.

I left the club as quickly as I could—into Chinatown and its everything. Being an asshole, I was actually looking for a cake for Matt. It was his birthday, and the promoter, Max, had arranged for a notoriously beautiful Lower East Side lass in a schoolgirl uniform to deliver a surprise and a cake on stage. I agreed to get the cake.

Cutting a roundabout heading for Little Italy, I ran into Lenny, on his way to the club to check on things. He was approaching the end of his rope with us but was a professional. He offered to pay for the cake, which meant I could afford to stop somewhere for a beer, and then everything with decent baked goods was closed. The cake wound up being Entenmann's from the Food Emporium. Nonetheless, we bought some trick candles and headed back.

Feathers

The dressing room scene at the Bowery was a cockfight. Shannon of the Heroin Sheiks had come straight from the haberdashery *more* disappointed with the world he chose to observe from under a hat. Guest-listed friends jockeyed for beer and wet tortilla chips. Some German women

smoked disapprovingly and talked of *men* and their *guitars.*
Always people dropped things.

Matt's family was there. A woman in the entourage, who
decided that my returning accompanied by Lenny was proof
of a conspiracy, draped herself over Matt's mother (with
whom I had spent innumerable pleasant Christmases) and
announced through whore makeup that they were "the
same," and they would unilaterally "kick my ass" if I
"tried any fuckin' shit." Matt's mother looked uncomfortable. I dumped the cake in the office and went to the balcony bar.

People who would know, people we all trust, say
unequivocally that it was the best show we had ever
played. Appropriately, it was our last.

At the end of the night, there was a scene outside the
Bowery with equipment smashed in the middle of
Delancey Street. Traffic screeched around it, honking.

A few days later, Eugene and I smoked by the pool and
said things and drank tequila and the greyhounds rolled in
the sun, and that was it.

12

Bookend

What the Hippopotamus Said

A kid, maybe three or so, burning up and down the aisle of the plane, has stopped at my row. He's decked out in sleeping gear meant to disguise him as a hippopotamus, and he stares at me. I have my little reading glasses on (years premature, but the damage is done); three scotches into the atmosphere, lightly rarified. After some silence has passed, I say hi. He runs off.

Soon he's back, breathing hard for a few seconds. "A lot of people say I'm good."

"Oh?"

"Yes. I go to bed well. And I'm active. I shop."

Here we go. "You shop?"

"Yeah. With Mommy."

"What do you shop for?"

"Oh, just things that we need. Like avocados, and . . ." Looking around the plane for closure, "And shoes."

"That's a fairly excellent hippo costume."

Nothing.

"You know where hippos live?"

Quietly, he says, "Darkest Africa."

Whoa! Fucking right! I'm jamming the call button ferociously for the drinks cart—kid's getting a bourbon.

The Morbid Stamp of the Buffet Culture

Today, decamping sober (kidding) at Tampa, choked in pur-
gatorial perfumes, half-deaf with no coffee, there are
people—all of them have their mouths open slightly. This
is not like a regular airport. There is much waddling about.
The air is heavy, fried, oppressive. Everywhere there is a
kind of pink shuffling. Stagnation, decay, and oh look.
Margaritas.

When one comes from Massachusetts to the orange juice
state or whatever it is called, in February, one is thankful for
each and every degree. I go around shining public ther-
mometers with my shirtsleeve, whistling and tipping my
hat. It's a great town, Florida is—they've got beer here and
everything, and if you can eat a hundred chicken wings in a
half-hour they name a church after you. Pelicans. Dowagers.
I'm here to relax. By which I mean drink. And if I get the
chance, which I imagine I will, do absolutely nothing. First,
I must get the rented "Sea Bring" safely over the bridge.

Loose in Atlantis

Pulled over the Bringer of Seas at a church to take a photograph of a fresh little sign on the lawn: "Cry Room," and
an arrow. Today, the cry room contained an estate, or
"rummage," sale. I bought a karate uniform for three
bucks, a wetsuit for ten, and most important, a linen suit
which fit perfectly and some white patent leather loafers.

It is possible on this island to avail oneself of a foolproof
hangover remedy in the form of a cocktail known opaquely
as The Nite Tripper. The drink is made with Kahlua,
Bailey's, and Frangelico. Not being a local, I have never
experienced a "local" hangover, but must imagine either
that the inventor of this curative has been hung to death as
a "fag," or that here there are a great many hypoglycemic

fishermen who do not know how to spot one. Relief comes in the same mouthful as a hamburger on a stick, brought forth from an un-refrigerated *box* near the door. This belies the original problem, and presents another one, in the form of the bad kind of poisoning. This is not a regular island. These people would be killed anywhere else. Take our man down the end. He has absolutely no idea what he is doing. Look at that. Jesus.

Close Calls

There was a fellow back in the pons asinorum days of hanging around the coffee shop who, upon hearing any reference to the state of Florida, would violently pleasure himself through his pockets. "HEY! DID YOU GUYS SAY SOM'N ABOUT FLORIDA?" Yes, this was prior to the years of sensitivity training, so we called him "Florida," with uniform results. While I do not quite share our man's enthusiasm, the accommodations are pretty good. A bit heavy on the wicker, but good. I can sit and type in the hanging gardens, like I am doing right now. Looking forward to getting to Marco's hut, sleeping on the beach, draped in seaweed tatters eating manta off a spear, relaxing dangerously in raw bars with his law partners—but this will do for a few days, certainly. The kitchenette is clean and has a good knife and the fishmonger is nearby.

In my head, I just bagged the whole thing. Everything. Cars, people, everything. Fuck it. Just walked down to the end of the pier and threw this piece of shit in to the sea, for starters. What does anybody really *need*? Health? Overly ambitious. What do *I* really need? Almost nothing, and I'm *soaking* in it. What's stopping me from a quiet life of monging fish?

Well, a quiet life of monging fish.

Twice: One time too many.

—*Ambrose Bierce*, The Devil's Dictionary

Still when I get home, I will shop for a van.

Picked up some incredible rum from a roadside stand. Retreating from the retreat. Florida's nice, but only for a few days.

The Golden Spike

Northampton, Mass.

Northampton is an incestuous *hive* of incest. Persons move around a set circuit. When the inertia gets critical, people go. As an asthmatic might relocate to drier and drier climates while failing to recognize the effects of a three-pack-a-day smoking habit, people are peeled off and re-stuck on backdrops across the country, still holding the beer from the last place. What were those called? Colorforms.

Everyone in this town has had each other's jobs, lovers, friends, guitars, apartments, clothing, colds, etc. Phases are contagious, and especially destructive ones. When ephedrine first became readily available at the Convenience Mart (that's what it's *named*. Goes to point.), everyone in town was a kangaroo with a pill maraca. All it takes is four people to start a two-month epidemic of rotten cocaine, two to get a scandal going, and the whole place takes a tumble if just one person gets either the flu or a record deal. Benders sort of make the rounds, but there are most definitely huge swaths of time when *everyone* is shit-faced *all the time*. Hundredth monkey? Try the third or so. Familiarity breeds—period.

I'm in a bar, for a change—"working," whatever anyone thinks. This is a bar I don't frequent. I came here to avoid certain distractions.

The other thing about Northampton, and I often forget this, is that it is the "Lesbian Mecca": confirmed by *The National Enquirer* even, a few years back. I'm not sure that any women elsewhere are kneeling on mats and murmuring towards our little dorp, but yes, there is considerable girl-on-girl action in these parts. I report this because two fed-up lesbians just got up from their stools and are now *beating the living shit* out of the mouthy ball-cap-wearing asshole who had been trying to pick them up—and because "She's A Lady," by Tom Jones, is on the jukebox.

It is what astronomers call "a moment."

Electrotrash

Same bar, two nights later. A wiry kid from Brooklyn is sloppy as hell. The pair of very attractive girls next to him wouldn't give him the time of day, but he persisted—sloppier and sloppier—until a bouncer decided to step in and yank him out of the bar by the collar. Choking in midair, the kid manages to blurt out rapidly, "Youguys wannacomeovermymom'shouseforChinesefood?" before he is tossed out the door.

World Is Fair

I don't remember even getting out of bed, but now I'm here in a peeling cattle hutch somewhere. It's been attacked with butcher paper and magic markers and onion ring grease. The lady in the stall to the left has got some sort of Aryan vacuum cleaner business going, and is going on in halting Polish about things getting "cleaner," and vacuuming fat little handfuls of popcorn off a throw rug. The guy on the other side is selling maps of local rock formations. No one around looks approachable for pills of any kind.

This is a farm town of maybe a couple thousand. It ekes out a fire department and a seasonal library by having a pumpkin army and American flags everywhere, and once a year, this little party. *The Fair*: arts, crafts, rides, fried things; alcoholic magicians and their ex-wives who get sawed and then magically slapped while they stand there part-way out of their sequins; firemen and puppets (both drunk); wood shapes stenciled with cruel aphorisms about home and family; mason jars and doilies with needlepoint. There's a guy selling tapes of Celtic music and, I think he said, Traditional Christmas Porn—either that or Celtic porn, which is even less likely. There is a sizable pig and goat-touching area for the children, and only slightly separated is the area for eating them with sauerkraut. All is judged: carrots, rope, pies, cows. But in truth, a cow cannot be judged. It stands there big as a minivan, droopily re-chewing the contents of one of its many stomachs, swatting flies with its tail, defiantly conjuring two-thirds of a White Russian six inches from its ass. Meanwhile, the judges can't whistle while pissing. I will add here that the Fair is dry. *Dry.* Ribbons stuck everywhere. Country music comes out of everything. There's a guy playing a saw, then a barbershop quartet, then a polka. A stuffed monkey in a little remote controlled jeep goes around a track in a pen, chasing a goose.

The lumberjack competition is excellent. Paul Bunyans come from all over New England to chop, to shred—to lumberjack-off. They turn a log into a grape trellis in one minute, or they just hack the thing into an olive pick in thirty seconds with a battle-axe. Emcee Woodsman's got a microphone and he's keeping everyone posted. He's clearly done this before. He may be a respected local now, but there's no way he isn't from Lawrence or Revere. Luckily, whether by birth or barroom wager, one of the competitors is called Marcus Auralius. *And heah comes Mahcus Arayleeus and I think he wahnts a peece a tha pie. Am I right, Mahcus? Mahcus Arayleeus hails frum New Bedfahd, Ladies and Genlemen. Mahcus could build yoo an ahk between thundahclaps, and yoo should see him on the Roto Tillah, people. Em eye rite, Mahcus?* Marcus doesn't say shit; he just starts up the chainsaw.

It's a princely fourteen bucks to get into the Fair, if you don't want to wade through water and climb a fence. Then they rape you for a lemonade, turn you out on some kind of fried river clam, and lash you to a giant demented swinging ride operated by Ed Gein. It's quite beautiful, actually, but I shouldn't be here. I'm struggling to stand in a horse stable that has been temporarily converted into a walk-up domestic abuse information booth. On the walls are some shaky therapeutic hand tracings with upsetting phrases on them. One scrawl reads, "I never do anything right." Someone else's arrow and pink bubble letters read: "Me neither!"

My job, as I barely understand it, is two-fold. The main attraction is some sort of hastily painted wooden emotional prize wheel. I am supposed to invite folks to spin this. It lands on a purple slice that says "Support" and then you get a balloon. "Peace at Home" is another slice, and another balloon. Little pointer lands on "Unconditional

Love," and there you go. All set—you get a balloon. The traditional little carnival tommy guns would have been more cathartic for everyone probably, but one has what one has, and what one has today is a hangover and a Wheel of Misfortune. *Step right up, step right up! Win one for the lady? You look like a victim! Have a balloon!* People pass, mostly, as the wheel doesn't know *what it's like*. At one point, an enormous old woman in a yellow muumuu with two granddaughters comes up, asking for extra balloons and fuck the wheel, she's got to get these kids out of New York and away from their father (which they already visibly are). But I apologize, because I don't have enough balloons to get anyone out of New York. Where it stops, nobody knows.

Though these helium tanks here are loosely related to tanks of certain better and more intoxicating gasses with which I am already familiar (this is actually a reason why, I am told, I was chosen for the job over qualified social workers and people who regularly get up early), the inflation technique was explained to me while a bit of coke fell from my nose onto a book about cheesemaking. I gather this was one of the prizes. The book, I mean. I don't know how one would go about winning it, or why after being attracted to the domestic violence booth, one would be comforted by this book. Or by me: dressed completely in black, sunglasses smashed into my face, in agony. Why I am here at this point is irrelevant. Sometimes it is not about asking the right questions.

It was later suggested that I get on a particular ride, a thing of blinking glitter and the phrase "Crazy Boat" written in bulbs. The vessel, of very debatable seaworthiness—though assuredly crazy—is mostly empty but for some fearless seven-year-olds and an unescorted fat man with a candied apple. There's a confident little girl sitting next to me and I need some answers.

"So how does this thing . . . um, go?"

"What?"

"I mean, when it starts, where does it go?"

"Up."

A giant metal bar slams down, trapping everyone. It's exactly two-thirty because I can see, through the last of the choking old-time car parade, Smokey the Bear emerging from his trailer directly across. I had noticed earlier that he was scheduled to arrive at two thirty. He is accompanied by a number of forest rangers and State Troopers. The little event board didn't say anything about cops. Let alone twenty of them.

"Oh. Just up?"

"No. And down. *Duh.*"

"Uh huh. I see. Is it scary?"

"*No.*"

This was bullshit. A buzzer went off, and the Crazy Boat was swung up into the air with a tremendous jerking motion, as if you were being chiropracted by a vengeful, drunken whale. You saw the treetops and the rolling fields for a few seconds, and then were yanked back towards the ground and dragged helplessly past twenty cops and a rule-making bear, and then cannonballed back into a languorous blue sky.

Subsequence for Consequence

> *"It's an ending. That's enough."*
>
> —*Marge Simpson*

It used to be, however many years ago, that when I put the band name into a search engine (the computer kind), the results would consist mostly of instructions for unwrapping things, broccoli in particular.

I considered asking a total stranger to summarize the fall of The Unband, provided he had never heard of it. Exhaustion, conspiracy, tornado, booze, lists, women, money, shake-ups at mega-corp, artistic differences, druggings, the giant inflatable Hand of Fate. It's the same story, even when the most important part is that it isn't. Anyone could tell it cold. That's the whole joke right there:

Guy walks into a bar.

EPILOGUE

Breaking It Down Like Animal House

Parties who were not in or around the band during its death throes—or during the year that followed, in which accidental meetings of band members in the streets of Northampton or New York resulted always in screaming matches where people held back other people from the brink of prison sentences, resulting in communitywide action to keep everyone apart by means of lookouts and secret entrances and exits and disguises—have casually expected the band to get back together. This has not come to pass.

However, the ravages of time take their toll on even the stateliest of revenge fantasies. No one's screaming or punching each other anymore. Though it is silently acknowledged that it is best to keep the conversation fairly light, all band members and crew, and many or even most associates, are at the time of this writing perfectly capable of having a beer and laughing in each other's company.

Matt: *Recently promoted to head manager of Personal Care Agency in Northampton. Plays guitar and sings in reconstituted Fistah (former Unband alias). Resides in quiet residential neighborhood in Western Massachusetts among superb works of art depicting dogs with eerily human faces. Has his health, 2002 Acura.*

Eugene: *Gainfully employed by forensics branch of the Federal Bureau of Investigation, Smith College division (removed from broader duties due to his regularly being assigned to investigate himself and blowing cover). Resides in the hills outside Northampton. Plays guitar and sings for the Probates, and drums and drinks for Million Drink March. Still sleeps well. Has his health, six-pack abs.*

Mike: *Lost mind, other things in small office space in Northampton during endless sleepless winter storm of wine and "pep" pills, while assembling book about defunct unknown band. Perfected method of opening cans of vegetarian baked beans with a hammer, windowsill. Resides in the hills outside of town with Eugene. Plays guitar and sings in Million Drink March. Currently over-thinking finishing touches on Million Drink March record. Has his health, pending departure of talking raven.*

Mink: *Of his two guitars, Push and Pull, one hung on the wall of the Hard Rock Café Boston, in rightful company between Eddie Money's police uniform and Pete Townshend's nose warmer, until he stole it back after losing remaining guitar navigating rapids in private Amazon. Resides outside of Boston, where he is one half of the classic and futuristic radio morning team of himself on a popular soft-rock station.*

Steve: *Resides in Northampton. Plays guitar and sings for ceaselessly touring beer band, Drunk Stuntmen: beloved by No Depression, bikers, belles of the ball at annual fish-throwing contest in the Gulf of Mexico. Has his health, magical cowboy hat.*

Safety Bear: *Resides safely in Benanjerry, Vermont. Has his health, tools, ball cap.*

A feature-length documentary film about the Unband is in the editing stage at an undisclosed location in the New Mexico desert.